CIVIL WAR
SCHEMES AND PLOTS

Webb Garrison

Gramercy Books
New York

This 2001 edition is published by Gramercy Books™,
an imprint of Random House Value Publishing, Inc.,
280 Park Avenue, New York, New York 10017,
by arrangement with Rutledge Hill Press.

Random House
New York • Toronto • London • Sydney • Auckland
http://www.randomhouse.com/

Printed and bound in the United States of America

A CIP catalog record for this book is available from the Library of Congress.

ISBN 0-517-16287-3

8 7 6 5 4 3 2 1

Contents

Part 4: Nipped in the Bud

Part 5: Much Ado about Nearly Nothing

Part 6: Flood Tide of Fraternal Strife

Preface

DIFFICULT SITUATIONS FOSTER EXPERIMENTATION. Desperate situations encourage daring. Impossible situations demand that something new under the sun must be conceived and tried.

For four years following April 1861, the thirty-four states that earlier had tried to form "a more perfect union" included few disinterested citizens. From ordinary men and women to general officers in blue and in gray, virtually everyone was totally enmeshed in the North-South conflict.

With so many people trapped in desperate situations, it was inevitable that a lot of wildly varied enterprises should be hatched. Some of them—such as a plan to set anthracite coal mines on fire to force Federal warships to burn bituminous coal and emit clouds of black smoke—withered on the vine.

Many other schemes ripened and went through unplanned changes as they were nurtured to maturity. It was inevitable that the majority of them, whether developed within the Union or by the Rebels, should have little or no impact upon the bloody struggle.

Yet a handful of these products of creative minds in desperate times not only succeeded after a fashion, they represent landmark achievements in Western civilization. The Civil War was the seedbed in which "the mother of all little games" took root and flourished.

The importance of a venture was not a criterion in selecting a subject to be treated in this book. Neither was its success or failure. Simple human interest was the sole factor. Thus pure reading pleasure is the objective of this volume, and if you also learn a bit about our nation's history, so much the better!

Part 1

Best-laid Plans

FRANK LESLIE'S ILLUSTRATED WEEKLY

Gold speculators in New York.

1

The Great Gold Hoax

Greed and the 1864 Draft

NEW YORK SUBSCRIBERS TO the *Journal of Commerce* and the *World* stared in astonishment at the announcement carried by their newspapers on May 18, then many of them exploded with anger.

Executive Mansion
May 17, 1864

Fellow Citizens of the United States:

In view of the situation in Virginia, the disaster at Red River, the delay at Charleston, and the general state of the country, I, Abraham Lincoln, do hereby recommend that Thursday, the 26th day of May, A.D., 1864, be solemnly set apart throughout these United States as a day of fasting, humiliation and prayer.

Deeming furthermore that the present condition of public affairs present an extraordinary occasion, and in view of the pending expiration of the service of (100,000) one hundred thousand of our troops, I, Abraham Lincoln, President of the United States, by virtue of the power vested in me by the Constitution and the laws, have thought fit to call forth, and hereby do call forth, the citizens of the United States between the ages of (18) eighteen and (45) forty-five, to the aggregate number of (400,000) four

> hundred thousand, in order to suppress the existing rebellious combinations, and to cause the due execution of the laws.
>
> And, furthermore, in case any state, or number of states, shall fail to furnish, by the fifteenth day of June next, their assigned quotas, it is hereby ordered that the same shall be raised by an immediate and peremptory draft.

Just ten months earlier, the largest city in the nation had been wracked by the worst draft riot on record. Now "the Illinois Baboon" had the nerve to call for a new draft!

There was no doubt that the Union military effort had bogged down and more men were needed to replace casualties and those whose terms of enlistment were expiring. Taken collectively, however, the bits of dire news in the presidential proclamation seemed to spell disaster.

Gold, long considered the safest of investments in times of great trouble, shot up on the exchange. At one point during that day, the price was 10 percent above that of May 17, and when the exchange closed, it showed a gain of 8 percent. Obviously, someone with insider knowledge could have gained financially.

Subscribers to the city's four other newspapers did not read the story in their papers; it appeared that the *World* and the *Journal of Commerce* had scored a great scoop. The employees of the *Tribune* knew that Horace Greeley's newspaper had also published the story but did not distribute it. After an early press run, the editors concluded that the presidential proclamation was a hoax, so they destroyed twenty thousand copies.

Maj. Gen. John A. Dix, commander of the military Department of the East, was alarmed at the news that broke on "steamer day" and believed the proclamation to be spurious. Within a few hours ships would sail bearing the news abroad, he informed Washington by telegraph, requesting immediate confirmation or denial.

Received at the War Department at 11:35 A.M., the Dix inquiry brought an immediate response from the secretary of war, Edwin M. Stanton, who branded the proclamation "a base and treasonable forgery." Simultaneously, Secretary of State William H. Seward sent messages to the New York press and to the U.S. ambassadors in London and Paris, Charles Francis Adams and William L. Dayton.

Stanton also telegraphed Maj. Gen. Lew Wallace in Baltimore to seize all copies of the *World* and the *Journal of Commerce* that reached

Secretary of War Edwin M. Stanton.

the city "by express or mail . . . and report to this Department." Hours later, Wallace informed him that papers carrying the proclamation had arrived by train and were distributed before he received his orders. "I have seized all the copies I could find," he concluded.

Some time after noon, Abraham Lincoln ordered General Dix to arrest "the editors and proprietors and publishers" of the *World* and the *Journal of Commerce,* holding them "in close custody until they can be brought to trial before a military commission." Lincoln also instructed Dix to "take possession, by military force, of the printing establishments of the New York World and Journal of Commerce and hold the same until further orders, and prevent any further publication therefrom."

Stanton dispatched another telegram in which he directed Dix to "take military possession of the offices of the Independent Telegraph Company." He was to seize "instruments, dispatches and papers" and arrest "the manager, operators, and superintendent."

Late in the afternoon, Dix informed Washington that the fraudulent document had been delivered by hand to the offices of the city newspapers at 4:00 A.M., when "none of the responsible editors was present." He further noted that the bogus proclamation was "written on thin manifold paper of foolscap size, like the dispatches of the associated [*sic*] Press. In handwriting and every other respect it was admirably calculated to deceive."

While writing his dispatch, Dix received the president's order to arrest the personnel of the offending newspapers. Hence he ended his message by saying, "I shall execute [that order] unless the foregoing information shall be deemed sufficient by the President to suspend it until my investigation is concluded."

Stanton replied, "The President's telegram was an order to you which I think it was your duty to execute immediately upon its receipt." As a result, at 5:40 P.M. the War Department received a telegram from Dix saying that he would act immediately to seize the telegraph offices, newspapers, and editors.

Another telegram from Stanton scolded Dix for having offered to investigate. His duty was simply to do as instructed, with investigations to be made by a military commission, said the secretary of war. At 8:30 P.M., two hours later, he informed Dix that the forged proclamation probably originated in New York and "publishers were not privy to it."

At 2:30 P.M. on May 19, Lincoln received a telegram signed by the executives of four New York newspapers: the *Tribune, Express, Herald,* and *Sun.* They explained that "any ingenious rogue" could have perpetrated the hoax and respectfully requested that the president rescind "the order under which the *World* and the *Journal of Commerce* were suppressed."

The following day Dix notified Stanton: "I have arrested and am sending to Fort Lafayette Joseph Howard, the author of the forged proclamation. He is a newspaper reporter, and is known as 'Howard,' of the Times. He has been very frank in his confession—says that it was a stock-jobbing operation." Howard, age thirty-five and working as city editor of the *Brooklyn Eagle,* exonerated the Independent Telegraph Line and everyone except Francis A. Mallison, a young reporter for the *Eagle,* who had been persuaded to "duplicate an Associated Press dispatch" and then distribute it to Manhattan papers.

The confessions of Howard and Mallison should have ended the great gold hoax, but they did not. Secretary of the Navy Gideon Welles, a former newspaper editor, wrote: "The seizure of the office of the *World* and *Journal of Commerce* for publishing this forgery was hasty, rash, inconsiderate, and wrong, and cannot be defended. . . . The act of suspending these journals, and the whole arbitrary and oppressive proceedings, had its origins with the Secretary of State."

Throughout the nation—even in occupied New Orleans—newspaper editors generally voiced the sentiments that Welles later

HARPER'S WEEKLY

Joseph Howard, perpetrator of the ingenious scheme.

expressed. With Lincoln facing what seemed to be an uphill battle for reelection, much of the blame for the arrests and suppressions rested on him.

Heavily Democratic, New York was in an uproar. Gov. Horatio Seymour ordered the district attorney to prosecute Dix before a local magistrate. City judge A. D. Russell heard lengthy arguments in the case of *The People* vs. *John A. Dix and Others* but refused to make a definitive ruling.

Howard's father, a member of the church pastored by Henry Ward Beecher, persuaded his minister to intercede for the forger. As a result Beecher's close friend, Lincoln, arranged for the release of the framer of the gold hoax.

Precisely two months after the bogus draft proclamation was printed, the president signed a proclamation calling for five hundred thousand volunteers. Like the Howard document, it called for a draft in every political entity that failed to fill the quota assigned to it under the call.

Not until long afterward did anyone outside the circle of Lincoln's intimate advisers see another document. Signed on May 17, 1864, it called for the draft of three hundred thousand men "to increase the active and reserved forces of the Army, Navy, & Marine Corps of the United States."

Cities, towns, and wards were given until July 1 to fill their quotas by raising volunteers; after that the draft was to go into effect. This order seems to have been deliberately omitted from the *Official Records,* where the bogus proclamation framed by Howard appears in full. Roy Basler, editor of *The Collected Works of Abraham Lincoln,* theorizes that the gold hoax caused this suppression.

In 1864 Union forces faced a manpower shortage that was rapidly becoming critical. Under an act of February 24, only 14,741 drafted men were examined. Of these, 7,016 were exempted and 5,050 paid commutation money. As a result, this Union call for men netted only 1,675. The results of the draft of 1863 had been slightly better but were far below expectations. Although the "quota actually drafted for" was 194,962, only 88,137 men were obtained. These results suggest that Lincoln's proclamation of May 17—never issued because of the Howard hoax—was designed merely to fill gaps in the ranks, rather than to increase the total size of Union forces.

On May 18, when Lincoln's genuine proclamation was withheld because of Howard's hoax, Washington did not know that about eighteen thousand more Federal casualties were being added in the Spotsylvania Court House campaign that ended May 19. In battles from the Wilderness to Cold Harbor, more than fifty thousand gaps appeared in Union lines; because of the bogus proclamation, these gaps were not filled for months.

For two crucial months Ulysses S. Grant and his generals pleaded for men in vain because a greedy newspaper writer pulled off a hoax to make for himself an undetermined profit from the one-day jump in the value of gold.

2

King Cotton

A World Monopoly

Writing in the *National Intelligencer* on April 5, 1854, R. E. Scott addressed a warning to northern readers. There was no need to voice his views in the South. Most persons where cotton was king already held that general view as an article of faith.

> Wherever slavery prevails, capital and labor will be mainly employed in the business of agriculture. In this country it has devoted the immense territory of fourteen States to the growth of raw materials for commerce and manufactures. Merchants, mechanics, farmers, lawyers, doctors, in a word, every professional and industrial pursuit, derive profit from [slavery]. Deprive Great Britain of the fruits of her commerce in our staples, and she would be almost stricken from the list of independent states; without them she could not clothe and give employment to her thronging masses, nor long stagger under the weight of her accumulating debts. Deprive the great cities of Boston, New York, and Philadelphia of these fruits, and their huge proportions would fall to decay, and scenes of wretchedness more absolute than words could depict mark their ruin.

New York financial analyst T. M. Kett was busy compiling data that he eventually put into a book called *Southern Wealth and Northern*

Profits. Much of the volume, as well as numerous other economic analyses, centered upon a single agricultural product—cotton—which was the chief asset of the United States in international trade.

Ten years before the birth of Abraham Lincoln, total exports of the nation barely topped $71 million, of which cotton accounted for just 7 percent. Four decades later exported cotton alone brought a return to the nation of $63 million. During the next twenty years the return rose sky-high, to about $191 million. This meant that in the troubled era just before the outbreak of war, cotton accounted for nearly 60 percent of the value of all American exports.

Shipping and manufacturing industries were erected on the foundation laid by immense crops of raw cotton. First in England and later in the United States, power-driven machines spun more and more thread, then wove increasing quantities of fabric to clothe much of the world's rapidly growing population. British mills alone consumed an estimated 700 million pounds of cotton annually, with at least 85 percent of it coming from the American South.

Although cloth was made by machines, in the production of raw cotton only the final process of separating fibers from seeds was done by machine, Eli Whitney's gin or one of its many adaptations. Plowing, planting, tending, and harvesting—or picking—were totally dependent upon hand labor. Thus Sen. Robert Toombs of Georgia and other spokesmen for the South could boast that without slave labor much of the world would go naked.

The price of cotton was loosely linked to the quantities produced. With the 1845 crop yielding less than two million bales, the price jumped to sixteen cents per pound. Just three years later, a crop of nearly three million bales brought the cotton farmer just over four cents per pound. This situation led to a series of annual Southern Commercial Conventions, whose announced goal was to see that cotton never dropped below ten cents per pound.

Even at six cents per pound, any man who owned at least three thousand acres and fifty slaves was on the road to wealth. Although plantation owners constituted a small minority of citizens in the Cotton Belt, these aristocrats held the political power.

Individually and collectively, they agreed that since the South had a world monopoly on cotton production, it would be to their interest to separate from the North and make even more money from cotton. After secession, the Confederate leaders believed that foreign demand

ILLUSTRATED LONDON NEWS

Unemployed cotton-mill workers in Manchester, England, apply for free food.

for the fiber would lead to quick recognition of the Confederacy as an independent nation.

Poor whites of the region, who worked for eighty cents a day, didn't own slaves. Hinton R. Helper of North Carolina pled their case in a highly inflammatory booklet, *The Impending Crisis.* Slave labor, he argued, cut the wages of white working men; as a result he predicted an economic crisis for the region.

Frederick Law Olmsted, who later distinguished himself as the planner of New York's Central Park, made a leisurely journey through the cotton-producing region. He then echoed Helper's views by denouncing slavery as an evil—economic rather than social. He was right in saying that the system fostered the abandonment of farm land after about seven years, soaked up capital needed for buildings and roads, and discouraged free labor.

Helper was denounced throughout the South, and Olmsted was ignored. Every cotton grower knew that yields were rising steadily as a result of better seeds and plows. Abolitionists could make all the noise they wished, but it remained the conviction of both the common man and the plantation owner that cotton would defeat all external efforts to make changes.

Throughout the region, newspapers annually reprinted—often in boldface type—lines credited to an 1855 address delivered in Columbia, South Carolina: "Should they make war on us, we could bring the whole world to our feet. . . . What would happen if no cotton was furnished for three years? . . . England would topple headlong and carry the civilized world with her. . . . No, you dare not make war on cotton. No power on earth dares make war on it. . . . COTTON IS KING."

That cotton was king was an article of faith even to small southern farmers. Coupled with sectional pride, it persuaded men who had little or nothing to gain from secession to support the movement. Many a dirt farmer was to fight the Yankees because he believed, correctly, that once cotton left the gin house, vast profits from handling and processing it went to the North.

Most of the cotton shipped to England and France was carried in northern-owned ships. After 1850 most of the big cotton mills were in the North, where banks lent money and handled international transactions for fat profits. Northern manufactured goods flooded the South, hauled to the region by railroads operating under a rigged system of rates. To make matters worse for the agricultural South, the industrial North had sufficient political clout to impose high tariffs on the imported goods needed in the region of few factories.

Most posturing and a great deal of activity whose goal was the creation of a separate southern nation came from the faithful subjects of King Cotton. By keeping its stranglehold on the world's supply, they believed they could maintain their monopoly, create their own big banks and import-export houses, send their cotton across the seas in southern-owned vessels, and abolish those outrageous tariffs.

Augustus B. Longstreet, president of a Georgia college destined to grow into Emory University, addressed a volume of "letters" from his state to Massachusetts in which he insisted that he loved the Union, but there were clear signs that the Union would prove to be a golden calf. He predicted Georgia would overthrow the Union as readily as Moses had overthrown Aaron's golden calf.

Longstreet's audacious book went through eight editions. Newspapers quoted widely from it, while political orators cited his arguments and amplified them. No doubt about it, they repeated over and over, cotton really rules!

LIBRARY OF CONGRESS

A relatively small riverboat brought 9,226 bales of cotton to New Orleans.

Savannah's booming cotton exchange was challenging London for recognition as the world's largest. Warehouses and docks at New Orleans, Savannah, Charleston, and many smaller ports bulged with four-hundred-pound bales headed overseas. In London, the editors of the *Times* condensed the matter into two sentences: "The destiny of the world hangs on a thread. Never did so much depend upon a mere flock of down!"

Once South Carolina led the secession parade and Lincoln reacted by calling for troops, a showdown was inevitable. At first, it appeared that cotton would triumph, for the 1860 crop topped 4.5 million bales. After First Bull Run, New Orleans shipped cotton worth $92 million and established a world record. Northern textile magnate William Sprague swapped huge quantities of arms and munitions for Confederate fibers. In England the humor magazine *Punch* summarized the international situation in doggerel:

> Though with the North we sympathize
> It must not be forgotten
> That with the South we've stronger ties
> Which are composed of cotton.

Moving to exploit their most valuable commodity, Confederate lawmakers took a series of steps. Seeking to withhold cotton from the market and boost its price, they imposed an export tariff. Soon cotton became the collateral used in seeking and gaining money from abroad, notably the Erlanger loan of $14.5 million that in 1862 was floated largely by French interests. Eventually cotton was bartered for weapons, munitions, and supplies by the Confederate government. Some of this was among the estimated 540,000 bales shipped to England during the war years.

Problems surfaced quite early, however. Although no one in the South seemed to have realized it, both England and France had accumulated huge stockpiles of cotton. This meant that some of their mills could continue to operate even if no new bales crossed the Atlantic. Therefore, instead of rising sharply, prices began to drop.

After only a few months of war, food shortages became acute in much of the Cotton Belt. Individual states and later the Confederate government reacted by pleading with farmers to produce food instead of cotton. When voluntary measures proved ineffective, restrictions were imposed. Production dropped to three hundred thousand bales in 1864.

Before the end of 1861 some British analysts correctly predicted that King Cotton would soon find himself bound and helpless, with the Union eagle screaming for the kill.

PUNCH

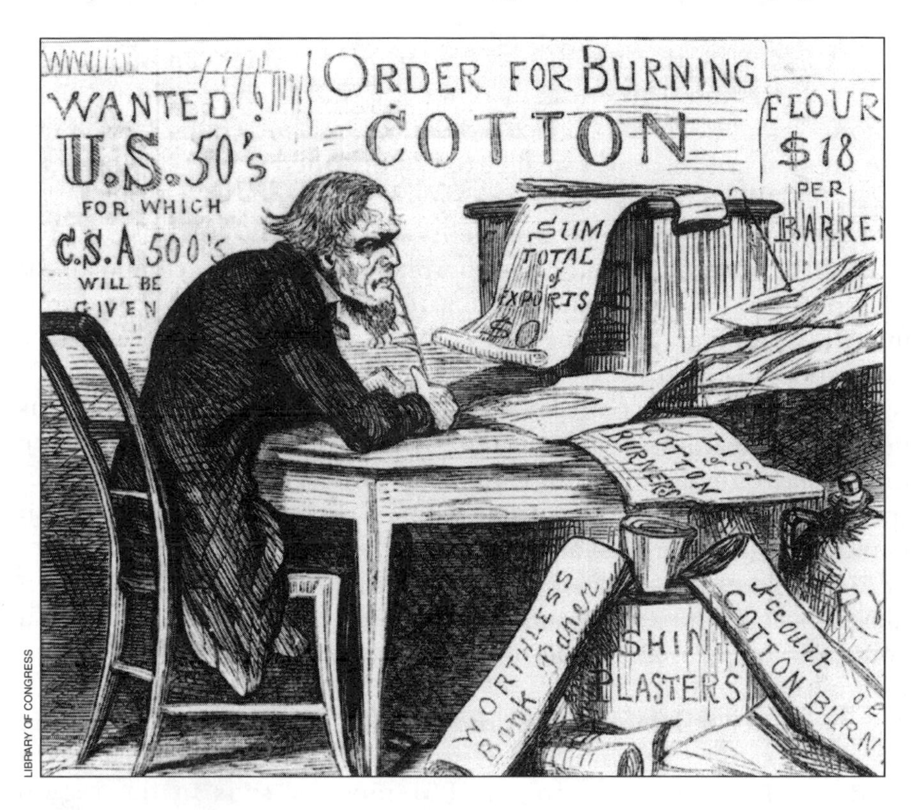

LIBRARY OF CONGRESS

While he fought rocketing inflation, a glum Jefferson Davis could not forget that he had ordered plantation owners across the South to burn any cotton likely to fall into Federal hands.

Much that was produced after 1861 was burned to prevent its seizure by Federal forces. Tens of thousands of bales were used in attempts to make "cottonclad" river boats impervious to enemy fire; huge stockpiles were quickly exhausted when cotton was employed to buttress earthworks and other fortifications.

To the chagrin of Southern growers and shippers, it was soon found that the Northern blockade could be evaded in more than one direction. Significant quantities of cotton found their way to Northern mills from Nassau. Some growers disposed of their crops at rock-bottom prices, only to see Northerners reap huge profits after having evaded the blockade or having smuggled cargoes through the lines. This flow of Southern fibers to the North was augmented by such commanders as Gens. Benjamin F. Butler and Nathaniel P. Banks through confiscation in Louisiana and Mississippi.

Worst of all, the diminished flow from the American South persuaded agricultural interests in other regions of the world to plant cotton. Egypt, India, and Mexico led the way, but vast cotton farms were also created in Russia and smaller ones flourished briefly in Northern states. Illinois led the way by producing one thousand bales in 1864.

Collectively, these developments spelled economic disaster for the South. Instead of being the triumphant holder of a trump card at the end of a victorious war, in 1865 the region found itself battered into the ground and offering cotton to the world at significantly lower prices than in 1860.

For generations cotton and slavery had gone hand in hand, as neither could flourish without the other. Since big operations were the most profitable, the number of slave owners gradually dropped in spite of a sharp rise in the number of slaves. It was the huge cotton plantation—not the one-family farm—that produced mythical hordes of happy slaves that were depicted in lithographs. At war's end, men like Robert Toombs were astonished to find that the defeated South could no longer make good use of newly freed blacks to keep King Cotton on his throne.

No other scheme on so grand a scale failed so miserably as did the South's effort to win political independence and financial might by depending on one crop. In 1861 most persons in the region regarded King Cotton as a benevolent monarch. Not until years later did his subjects see him as an ogre who was responsible for keeping the South dependent upon slave labor.

3

James J. Andrews

The Great Locomotive Chase

ALTHOUGH PRESIDENT JEFFERSON DAVIS was blind in one eye, he scanned documents so rapidly that few of them held his attention for more than two or three minutes. On a spring day in 1862 he began his customary hasty perusal of papers, then became so interested in a letter that he read it word for word.

Written in Atlanta on June 18, it was signed by Union soldiers from Ohio who were imprisoned in the Georgia railroad center. To the president of the Confederate States of America they introduced themselves as "survivors of the party that took the engine at Big Shanty [Georgia] on the 12th of April last."

Their civilian leader, James J. Andrews, and seven of their comrades had already been executed, they explained. "We all (with the exception of Andrews) were regularly detailed from our regiments in perfect ignorance of where we were going and what we were to do," they claimed.

After stressing their obedience to Andrews and their fidelity to duty, the prisoners addressed a poignant set of pleas to Davis:

> No real harm was done, and as far as thought and intention is concerned we are perfectly innocent. Oh, it is hard to die a disgraceful and ignominious death; to leave our wives, our children, our

brothers and sisters and parents without any consolation. Give us that mercy you yourself hope to receive from the Judge of all. We will all take an oath not to fight or do anything against the Confederacy. If this cannot be done at least spare our lives until the war is closed, if we have to remain in prison until that time.

Wilson W. Brown, William Bensinger, Elihu H. Mason,
John A. Wilson, John R. Porter, Mark Wood, Robert Buffum,
William Knight, William Pittinger, Daniel A Dorsey, Jacob Parrott,
William H. Reddick, M. J. Hawkins

If Davis replied to this petition, his letter was not preserved. Though sympathetic to the plight of these prisoners, he considered them to be spies and left their fate to military officials.

Nearly a year after the piteous plea addressed to Richmond went unanswered, Joseph Holt, the U.S. judge advocate general, framed a long report. Addressed to the secretary of war, Edwin Stanton, it gave the Federal version of a failed scheme known as Andrews's Raid.

In April 1862, wrote Holt, a party of noncommissioned officers and privates formed an expedition at the suggestion of J. J. Andrews of Kentucky. Operating "under the authority and direction of General O. M. Mitchel," he explained, twenty-two military volunteers, Andrews, and another civilian identified only as Mr. Reddick set out to wreck "the Georgia State Railroad between Atlanta and Chattanooga." The raiders expected to seize a locomotive and some cars, then "dash back in the direction of Chattanooga, cutting the telegraph wires and burning the bridges behind them as they advanced until they reached their own lines."

With Chattanooga, Tennessee, designated as their rendezvous site, the men who made up the raiding party bought civilian clothing to wear in the Confederate countryside. One of the raiders later insisted that he had used $125 of his own money for "a citizen's clothes, revolver, and expenses incurred while traveling."

Holt's account of the failed exploit noted that no raider wore his uniform, so the Rebels regarded each man as a spy. Two members of the party failed to reach their destination, but twenty-two arrived safely at Chattanooga.

From that rail center the would-be saboteurs "took passage for Marietta, Georgia, which they reached at 12 o'clock on the night of April 11." On the next morning they headed back north. At a place

GEORGIA DEPARTMENT OF ARCHIVES AND HISTORY

The most dramatic railroad chase of the war started at Big Shanty, Georgia, just north of Atlanta.

called Big Shanty, while the engineer and passengers were breakfasting, the raiders detached the locomotive and three boxcars from the train and started "at full speed for Chattanooga" on the line of the state-owned Western and Atlantic Railroad.

Andrews, who bragged that he left no detail to chance, had secured a railroad schedule and chosen April 12 because only one train was expected to be running south on the single-track line that day. To his dismay, the raiders had to pull aside to let at least four southbound trains pass. These delays cost them about an hour. Holt's report stated, "They removed rails, threw out obstacles on the road and cut [telegraph] wire from time to time, and attained when in motion a speed of 60 miles an hour, but the time lost could not be regained."

After having taken their stolen locomotive about one hundred miles to the north, the raiders ran out of wood, water, and oil. Then they saw a locomotive puff around a curve toward them. Hence, according to the official Federal account, "they had no alternative but to abandon their cars and flee to the woods, each one endeavoring to save himself as best he could."

Abandoning his legalese style, Holt then proceeded to wax almost poetic in his praise of the basic scheme: "The expedition itself, in the daring of its conception, had the wildness of a romance, while in the gigantic and overwhelming results which it sought, and was likely to accomplish, it was absolutely sublime."

Sublime or ridiculous, it failed absolutely because the twenty-six-year-old Western and Atlantic Railroad conductor William A. Fuller did not know when he was licked. Astonished to see his locomotive and two or three cars pull away from Big Shanty, Fuller tried to catch the runaways on foot. Failing, he took to a hand-powered construction car and then to a series of locomotives. The last one, called the *Texas,* he raced backward at speeds up to ninety miles per hour trying to catch up with Andrews and his men.

Almost before the big engine cooled off from its epic run, the captured raiders were thrown into jail in Chattanooga. Tried as a spy and found guilty, Andrews was executed in Atlanta on June 7. Twelve men were transferred to Knoxville, Tennessee. Seven who were arraigned before a court-martial were found guilty of engine stealing, bridge burning, and obstructing a railroad and were hanged on June 18.

The raiders failed in their objective as rain-soaked timbers refused to burn and not a single bridge was destroyed; however, their

"Captain" W. A. Fuller led the chase for the stolen locomotive.

ATLANTA HISTORICAL SOCIETY

GEORGIA DEPARTMENT OF ARCHIVES AND HISTORY

Before seven raiders were hanged simultaneously, one was permitted to address Confederate onlookers briefly.

dramatic attempt to cripple the Confederacy was celebrated long afterward in at least three movies. Kalem Studios released a silent one-reel film called *The Railroad Raiders of '62* in 1911; United Artists followed with *The General* in 1926; and in 1956 a highly successful Disney version of the story was called *The Great Locomotive Chase.*

The judge advocate's account pointed out that the man who initially received the most serious punishment was Pvt. Jacob Parrott of the Thirty-third Ohio Volunteers. Five Rebels took charge of him, and "without any form of trial bent him over a stone, and while two pistols were held over his head a lieutenant inflicted with a raw-hide upwards of 100 lashes on his bare back."

On the June day when seven of their comrades were executed, the fourteen survivors framed their futile plea to the Confederate White House. When they had heard nothing from President Davis by October, they attempted a jail break.

Col. J. M. Neibling, commanding officer of the Twenty-first Ohio Volunteers, described their escape in an 1863 report. The prisoners carved keys from meat bones to unlock their handcuffs and shackles. When a jailer came to collect their food dishes, they seized him and forced him to open all cell doors. Dividing into pairs, they set out in several directions.

They "were run by bloodhounds and shot at," Neibling said. "Traveling barefooted, sleeping in hollow logs, wet caves, and by traveling only at night with the North Star as their guide," five men reached their outfits. That's when Neibling wrote his account, designed to secure for them compensation for "loss of private moneys and equipments and for rations not drawn." Rations were included because standard-issue army food was considered part of a soldier's pay.

Six escapees who reached Washington by a circuitous route were given a special kind of compensation. In 1862 Congress had authorized the army Medal of Honor for enlisted men and amended it on March 3, 1863, to include officers. Secretary of War Stanton presented the first of these medals to Jacob Parrott and his five companions on March 24, 1863.

The concocter of the scheme, James J. Andrews, was a shadowy figure who seems deliberately to have concealed his past. Believed to have been a native of Virginia and perhaps to have been a house painter in early manhood, he moved to Flemingsburg, Kentucky, and launched a singing school.

Raider D. A. Dorsey, wearing the Medal of Honor.

UNIVERSITY OF GEORGIA LIBRARIES

Andrews clearly was foolhardy, but this little-known leader of one of the most action-packed nonmilitary raids of the Civil War exhibited altruism that has seldom been recognized. It is glimpsed only in some obscure papers sent from Flemingsburg, Kentucky, to Joseph Holt on March 31, 1863.

W. H. Cord, the county attorney, explained to Holt that he was acting "in the matter of the estate of James J. Andrews, deceased, a resident of this county." In mid-January David S. McGavic had appeared in court and sworn that he had known Andrews for more than a year prior to February 17, 1862, when Andrews confided to McGavic that "he was then in the secret military service of the Government of the United States, engaged in rather a critical business."

Andrews had given McGavic a check drawn on the Branch Bank of Louisville for twelve hundred dollars and told him, "I want you to draw this money out of bank, loan it out and the proceeds to go to the poor of Fleming County perpetually."

McGavic's only subsequent contact with Andrews was a letter written from Chattanooga on June 5, 1862, when Andrews knew he would go to the gallows in two days. In the letter, the adventurer gave a capsule account of the raid and instructed McGavic to "tell J. B. Jackson should there be any little claims that I neglected to settle to pay them and keep the horse. In regard to other matters [the check] do exactly as instructed before I left."

Andrews sent his regards to a Mr. and Mrs. Eckels, then ended his death-row message by writing: "According to the course of nature it will not be long until we shall meet in that happy country, the presence of the Lord. Blessed thought. Remember me also to the young ladies of Flemingsburg, especially to Miss Kate Wallingford and Miss Nannie Baxter."

There are no records concerning the source of the money that enabled Andrews's philanthropy by making an unrestricted gift equivalent to nearly eight years' pay for a Union private. This much, however, is beyond dispute: the obscure Virginian whose "perfect plan" was foiled by rain, unscheduled trains, and a determined Confederate railroad conductor did not conduct his raid purely for the sake of monetary reward.

4

Dr. Nightly

The Yellow Fever Plot

AN ASSISTANT SURGEON MADE the rounds of a Confederate hospital in Charleston, South Carolina. When he returned to his makeshift office, the doctor—who may have been James Evans—opened his ledger to the page on which a brigadier general's name was listed. Opposite "Smith, William D., B.G.," he scrawled just two words: "yellow jack."

In the fall of 1862 this constituted the medical verdict that death was certain and would come soon. Yellow fever, so named because it damaged a sufferer's liver and kidneys and caused the skin to turn brownish yellow, had been known in North America for 250 years.

Numerous port cities of the South experienced severe epidemics during the nineteenth century. Among them were New Orleans (widely called "the yellow fever capital"), Vicksburg, Natchez, Biloxi, Mobile, Memphis, Tampa, Pensacola, Galveston, Savannah, and Charleston.

In 1853 New Orleans had experienced one of the worst epidemics to hit North America. During five months of the summer and fall nearly half of the city's residents contracted the fever, but no accurate death toll was ever announced. Many young and healthy persons gradually recovered, but anyone over the age of thirty or who contracted yellow jack when exhausted had only a slim chance of survival.

LIBRARY OF CONGRESS

Because New Orleans was built on a sea-level delta, yellow fever was endemic.

Smith's illness was considered terminal as soon as the fever was recognized because for months he had worked or fought between fourteen and twenty hours a day and was weary to the point of exhaustion when he collapsed at his desk and was brought to the hospital. Born in Augusta, Georgia, in 1825, William Duncan Smith won an appointment to the U.S. Military Academy at West Point where his classmates included George B. McClellan and Thomas J. "Stonewall" Jackson. In the months prior to his death on October 4, 1862, Smith had been in charge of troops on James Island, south of Charleston Harbor. In June he had successfully held the fortified camp at Secessionville against a Union assault. When he became ill he was being considered to replace Maj. Gen. John C. Pemberton in command of the Department of South Carolina, Georgia, and Florida.

Had he been questioned, Smith's doctor would have said that there were a great many unanswered questions about yellow fever. No one knew why it seemed to select port cities as its targets, unless rats came ashore from seagoing vessels and somehow spread the disease. There was a possibility that yellow jack was caused by some invisible substance in the air that somehow spread from one victim to another. No one then realized, however, that the fever was transmitted by infected mosquitoes of a single variety, the *Aedes aegypti* mosquito.

Late in the fall of 1862 or very early in the winter of 1863, an unidentified physician was saddened to learn that Smith was gone. As he reflected on the way the fever had drained the life of a distinguished veteran of many battles, an idea slowly began to take shape.

Although the hero of Secessionville was the most recent Confederate general to die from yellow fever, other high-ranking officers had preceded him, as well as hundreds of privates and noncommissioned officers. Big bales of clothing worn by these victims had accumulated in port cities of the mainland and in the Caribbean Islands. In the cloth-scarce South these things were considered too good to discard but too dangerous to wear.

Why not put these contaminated articles to good use, reasoned the physician whose undercover name may have been "Dr. Nightly." At least that is the pseudonym that showed up in an occasional document relating to a top-secret plot. All persons who became involved in the elaborate scheme wanted their identities protected; if the idea should backfire, their lives would be in danger.

In theory their Yellow Fever plot was perfect. It would cost little to ship quantities of "infected clothing" to Northern cities and would require no skilled operatives. With the fever season of 1863 approaching, outbreaks of the disease caused by clothing taken from dead Confederates would inflict great losses in the ranks of the enemy.

Dr. Luke P. Blackburn is believed to have directed the Rebel scheme for germ warfare from Canada.

KENTUCKY HISTORICAL SOCIETY

Having suffered one delay after another, the plot appears to have been put into effect by Dr. Luke P. Blackburn, a native of Kentucky who practiced in Canada and went to Bermuda in 1864 to help fight an epidemic of yellow fever. Godfrey J. Hyams, a notorious turncoat who at times may have acted as a double agent, later testified that Blackburn entered into a contract with him. Under the terms of the 1864 agreement, Hyams said he was to be paid sixty thousand dollars to oversee the shipment of clothing and bed linens from yellow-fever victims to New York, Philadelphia, Norfolk, and other cities.

In his testimony before a Canadian court, Hyams added a footnote. One small valise entrusted to him held elegant shirts from which signs of "the black vomit" had been removed. His mission would not be completed until these shirts were presented to Abraham Lincoln.

Sketchy evidence suggests that at least one shipment of infected clothing reached Washington. Since the plot was developed and perhaps executed in what was supposed to be total secrecy, there are no reliable records concerning what was or was not done. There is no evidence, however, that yellow fever broke out in any Northern city as a result of the work by Hyams or other secret agents. If a substantial quantity of contaminated clothing was actually smuggled into Federal lines, it had no measurable effect.

DICTIONARY OF AMERICAN PORTRAITS

Dr. Walter Reed is credited with having conquered yellow fever long after the Civil War.

Forty years after the war, Dr. Walter Reed discovered that yellow fever was not spread by contact, but by a type of mosquito. Ironically, one of the men instrumental in the fight against yellow fever at the turn of the century, William Crawford Gorgas, was the son of the Confederate chief of the Bureau of Ordnance, Josiah Gorgas, and went on to be surgeon general of the United States.

Part 2

Genius at Work

BURT ENGRAVING

General Winfield Scott in his prime.

5

Winfield Scott

The Anaconda Plan

VIRGINIA-BORN GENERAL IN CHIEF Winfield Scott had such a reputation for looking after details that he was nicknamed "Old Fuss and Feathers." At age seventy-five, his body was beginning to deteriorate, but his mind was as keen as ever.

This fact did not escape the president-elect, Abraham Lincoln, who from his Springfield, Illinois, home began soliciting the views of the army's highest-ranking officer in the days following his November 1860 election. It wasn't until February 28, 1861, however, that he and Scott met personally.

That evening, Elbridge G. Spaulding, a congressman from New York, gave a private dinner at the National Hotel. As the guest of honor, Lincoln was seated close to Scott, and the two talked at length. Though many eastern newspapers derided the man they called "the Illinois Baboon," the Virginian concluded that Lincoln had "a capital mind." Soon Scott was preparing daily briefings for his commander in chief as the president's chief military adviser.

After the bombardment of Fort Sumter in April 1861, the need for a strategic plan was imperative. Very early in May, Scott confided to Maj. Gen. George B. McClellan that he had prepared what he considered to be the least bloody and most effective way to end the rebellion.

"Squeeze the Rebels . . . slowly," he proposed. "Make the recently announced blockade effective, and at the same time send flotillas of gunboats down the Mississippi River." When Federal forces had encircled the Confederacy, they could begin moving gradually inward. It would take time to get this done, but casualties on both sides would be light, and the South would eventually be strangled.

Scott regarded McClellan as a protégé and had no idea that the ambitious officer was planning to oust his chief and take his place. Behind Scott's back McClellan ridiculed what he called the old general's "boa-constrictor plan." Later, the press renamed the strategy after a different constricting snake, the anaconda.

Not knowing what was being said about him, Scott prepared detailed plans and presented them to the president. He urged that a force of at least sixty thousand men should be dispatched down the Mississippi River as soon as possible. By the time the great river was under Federal control "from Cairo, Illinois, to the Gulf of Mexico," he pointed out, the blockade would be effective.

Scott also raised one of Lincoln's favorite topics, Unionists within the Cotton Belt. They were outnumbered, the general conceded, but they could be found everywhere. Even Charleston, the seedbed of secession, included at least one prominent and outspoken opponent to secession. Great numbers of such folk could be found in eastern

MISSOURI HISTORICAL SOCIETY

Scott correctly saw the Mississippi River as the lifeline of much Southern commerce.

Tennessee and western North Carolina. If intelligence reports were accurate, there were pockets of Unionists in Alabama, Texas, and even Mississippi—the home state of the Confederate president.

Though presently almost silenced, Scott reasoned, Unionists in the South would gain in numbers and influence as living conditions worsened in the Confederacy soon to be suffering behind a full blockade. Even in the Cotton Belt, he said, this situation would lead the ordinary folk to turn against the political fire-eaters and wealthy slave owners who had fomented rebellion.

Lincoln did not formally reject the Anaconda Plan; he simply ignored it. When some details concerning the scheme were made public, newspapers and cartoonists lampooned it.

Yet barely six months after the Rebel victory at Bull Run, a handful of British and European analysts suggested that the Anaconda Plan seemed to have been put in motion. Port Royal, South Carolina, had been seized and converted into a major base for storing supplies and repairing warships. The reduction of Roanoke Island meant that much of coastal North Carolina would soon be under Federal control. If a significant move could be made in western waters, these commentators speculated, the Southern rebellion would be doomed.

No one in London or Paris knew that the secessionists had begun turning Columbus, Kentucky, into "a Gibraltar on the Mississippi." Soon its fortifications were so formidable that Federal use of the lower Mississippi River came to a halt.

Confederate leaders saw the necessity of drawing a defensive line from Columbus to the Cumberland Gap. To achieve this aim, it was essential to guard two major rivers that emptied into the Ohio. Fort Henry was established on the Tennessee River, and Fort Donelson was erected twelve miles to the east on the Cumberland River, which was navigable far to the south, beyond Nashville. Together, Forts Henry and Donelson seemed capable of blocking all Federal attempts to penetrate the western Confederacy by water.

At his Cairo, Illinois, headquarters, Commo. Andrew H. Foote pored over his maps and analyzed the latest intelligence reports. Before entering the U.S. Navy as a midshipman, he had studied at the U.S. Military Academy. With extensive experience in fighting pirates and slave traders, Foote lacked the inhibitions of many other high officers.

He enthusiastically supported the construction of a fleet of armored riverboats. By the time James B. Eads of Saint Louis was ready

HARPER'S WEEKLY

Long before the war ended, warships were more abundant on the major rivers in the South than on the high seas.

to deliver his vessels to the War Department, Foote believed he knew how best to use them.

When his plan was presented to Brig. Gen. Ulysses S. Grant, no persuasion was necessary. He'd readily put troops on transport vessels, said Grant, for a joint operation with Foote's gunboats. They could move down the Ohio and Tennessee Rivers to Fort Henry. Once it was conquered, Columbus or Fort Donelson would become the next objective.

A reconnoiter by gunboats, during which shots were exchanged, convinced the pair of Federal leaders to go into action in late January 1862. Foote planned to use four ironclad gunboats and a trio of wooden vessels. Collectively, his fleet mounted forty-nine guns—more than enough to deal with the estimated thirty-two guns at Fort Henry.

Manpower was a different matter. Crews would have to come largely from Grant's ranks because the navy was preoccupied with coastal action far to the east. Foote identified many experienced seamen among the army and had no difficulty getting permission to use them. Most units were under state control, however, and their elected captains and colonels balked at releasing men for river duty. Recruitment was attempted at points as far away as Chicago. In the end, Grant's soldiers were ordered to temporary ship duty by Maj. Gen. Henry W. Halleck, commander of the Department of the Missouri.

The Federal battle plan called for a simultaneous assault upon Fort Henry by Foote's gunboats and two divisions under Grant. Since the Confederate installation was known to include about four hundred log huts, it was believed to hold around fifteen thousand men. To protect it, numerous "torpedoes" (mines) were thought to be in the river.

More than five feet long and about one foot in diameter, a single torpedo could send a gunboat to the bottom. Holding about seventy pounds of powder, each device was equipped with prongs designed to fasten upon the bottom of a boat. Movable prongs were linked with triggers that would explode and ignite the powder.

Transports began landing Grant's troops three or four miles from their objective on February 4. On signal the Federals were to move rapidly on the fort as the gunboats went into action. Foote was gratified to find that most of the Confederate torpedoes were easily found and removed.

Early on the morning of February 5 scouts notified Confederate Brig. Gen. Lloyd Tilghman that the expected attack was imminent. After sending out additional scouts and patrols, Tilghman called his officers together. They had only 2,610 effectives to face an estimated 16,000 Yankees. Half of the men were untrained, and many carried flintlock muskets like those used in the War of 1812. Worse, only eleven of the fort's guns could be trained upon the river.

The Confederate command decided to offer a token resistance and send most of the troops to Fort Donelson. A handful would have to stay behind to slow the Federal advance and prevent the capture of retreating units. More than twenty-five hundred soldiers were transferred to Donelson on February 6, leaving sixty men to work Henry's guns. Two hours and ten minutes after the Federal assault began, with only four guns still serviceable, Tilghman surrendered. "The little garrison were prisoners," he later wrote. "But our army had been saved. We had been required to hold out an hour; we had held out for over two."

After the fighting was over the struggle seemed minor in scale. Just under one hundred Confederates became prisoners, sixteen of them being taken from a hospital boat in the river. Tilghman reported five men killed, eleven wounded, and five missing. Federal casualties were also light. On the steamer *Cincinnati* one man was killed and eight were slightly wounded. Capt. William D. Porter of the *Essex* was scalded by steam when a Rebel gunner hit the boiler of the warship.

Viewed from a distance, however, Fort Henry was seen as a major victory. Readers of the *Boston Journal* rejoiced to learn that a gate formerly closing the Tennessee River was now "open into the heart of the seceded states." Editors of the *Saint Louis Democrat* lauded the victory as "one of the most brilliant feats of the war."

At the site of the struggle, General Grant confined his first report to five short sentences that ended with a promise: "I shall take and destroy Fort Donelson on the 8th and return to Fort Henry." No official account of action on the Tennessee River mentioned General Scott, who had retired in November 1861 and been replaced as general in chief by McClellan. Old hands in both the army and navy nevertheless agreed that "at Fort Henry, the Anaconda Plan showed its worth."

That verdict proved to be correct. Fort Henry started the movement of the anaconda down the Mississippi River. Derided though it was when initially made public, Scott's scheme outlined the basic Federal movements that eventually squeezed the life from the Confederate States of America.

6

Stephen R. Mallory

Iron Afloat

CONFEDERATE SECRETARY OF THE Navy Stephen R. Mallory, formerly chairman of the U.S. Senate's Committee on Naval Affairs, had learned a great deal about sea-power innovations in Europe and Great Britain. Conversing informally with fellow lawmakers, he told them that "a great naval revolution is under way."

Mallory then explained that at Fort Constantine during the Crimean War, Russian guns made quick work of a fleet of British and French warships. That encounter convinced some naval authorities to experiment with vessels partially shielded with iron. Soon the French had the iron-protected *La Gloire* afloat, and the British put two partially armored vessels to sea, the *Warrior* and the *Ironside.*

When the U.S. Civil War started, the seceded states not only had no ships, they also had no sailors to man them. Practically all American commercial vessels of any size were owned and operated by northern investors. Although some officers and men of the U.S. Navy were considered certain to resign and fight for the South, in February and March 1861 only a few of them were in southern waters.

Mallory sent one of his aides to Yorktown, Virginia, where he found eighty experienced sailors in a single New Orleans regiment. Supplemented by seamen from Norfolk and other army units, more

HARPER'S ILLUSTRATED HISTORY OF THE GREAT REBELLION

Jefferson Davis (center) and his top advisers encouraged Mallory (seated, second from left) to try radical new ideas.

than three hundred volunteers were available to the Confederate navy, which as yet had no warships.

Under these circumstances, reasoned Mallory, he could not rely upon standard procedures and vessels. If he was to make any progress against the Northern navy, he would have to break new ground, taking great risks by experimenting with novel concepts. Thus on May 8, 1861, he wrote to members of the Navy Department:

> I regard the possession of an iron-armored ship as a matter of first necessity. Such a vessel at this time could traverse the entire coast of the United States, prevent all blockades, and encounter, with a fair prospect of success, their entire navy. Inequality of numbers may be compensated by invulnerability; and thus not only does economy but naval success dictate the wisdom and expediency of fighting iron against wood without regard to first cost. Not a moment should be lost. An agent will leave for England in a day or two charged with the duty of purchasing vessels.

James D. Bulloch, chosen to be the chief Confederate purchasing agent in Great Britain, was authorized on May 10 by the Congress to act on Mallory's proposal. He arrived in England on June 4 but soon found that no vessel of the sort described by the secretary of the navy could be purchased.

During the early months of the Confederacy other naval agents had scoured the waterfronts of New York, Philadelphia, and Baltimore, in search of wooden vessels suitable for war use. They had found only one such ship for sale, the *Caroline*—whose purchase was aborted by a violent clash between volunteer soldiers and civilians in Baltimore. Mallory's representatives fared no better in Canada, where on June 5 they ruefully reported that buyers sent by the U.S. government had beaten them to their targets.

As late as April 12, the day of the artillery duel in Charleston Harbor that ended with the surrender of Fort Sumter, the prospects seemed remote for securing a suitable steamer and converting it into an ironclad. Almost overnight, however, the situation changed drastically. Immediately after the firing on Fort Sumter, Abraham Lincoln and Gen. Winfield Scott had conferred about the possibility that the immense Gosport Navy Yard at Hampton Roads, Virginia, might fall into Confederate hands. Scott urged immediate precautionary action, but the president was hesitant to do anything that might affect public opinion in Virginia, which had not yet seceded.

When Virginia militia marched upon the installation on April 20, the Gosport commandant, Charles S. McCauley, decided to evacuate. Before leaving, he ordered the ships to be burned and sent squads of hand-picked men to blow up buildings.

The work of the demolition and fire crews was only partly successful. Some buildings escaped with only minor damage, and although nine burning vessels sent flames high into the air, some of them could be salvaged.

One of the warships badly burned but subject to restoration was the frigate USS *Merrimack*, aka the *Merrimac*. Built at the Boston Navy Yard at a cost of $685,842.19, the thirty-two-hundred-ton wooden screw-steamer had been launched on June 4, 1855. When she was torched, her five tubular boilers and two double-piston-rod horizontal condensing engines were badly worn. Although she was not quite six years old, the *Merrimack* had twice been out of commission for repairs. McCauley surely knew her condition, which could have influenced his decision to burn the warship instead of sending her hurriedly to another spot.

Still flaming, the *Merrimack* went to the bottom on April 20 about the time the navy yard was evacuated. When the secessionists examined her remains a day or two later, their engineers agreed that the damage was relatively slight and could be repaired fairly quickly.

Delighted to hear this, Mallory decided that the ship could be converted into the ironclad he desperately wanted. On July 18, he wrote, "The frigate Merrimac has been raised and docked at an expense of $6,000, and the necessary repairs to hull and machinery to place her in her former condition is estimated by experts at $450,000."

Having decided to shield the salvaged vessel with enough iron to make her ball-proof, Mallory requested and received from the Confederate Congress a special appropriation of $175,523. In spite of the scarcity of funds, the secretary of the navy had advanced a convincing argument: "Iron-clad steamships capable of resisting the crushing weight of projectiles from heavy ordnance must at an early day constitute the principal part of the fighting vessels of all naval powers."

The conversion and equipment of the *Merrimack* constituted a task of such magnitude that Mallory divided it into three areas and placed an experienced officer in charge of each. Naval constructor John L. Porter was ordered to cut the vessel down and submerge her end, "originating all the interior arrangements by which space can be economized." Lt. John M. Brooke was to secure iron and guns. William P. Williamson, chief engineer of the navy, obtained and transported to Norfolk the necessary machinery to propel the converted warship, whose name was changed to the CSS *Virginia.*

Metal of the type and quantity needed could be produced at only one place in the Confederacy, the Tredegar Iron Works in Richmond. After extensive tests, Brooke decided to use iron two inches thick, placing the underlayer horizontally and the upper vertically. The sheets were bolted through the vessel's thick woodwork and clinched inside. Though her pilothouse was protected, the rudder and propeller were not.

Brooke designed and the Tredegar Works produced two seven-inch rifled guns of a type never before seen. Each was reinforced around the breech with steel bands three inches thick, which were shrunk into position. One went into the bow and the other into the stern of the *Virginia.* Her additional firepower consisted of two similar six-inch guns and six nine-inch smoothbores that were mounted along the port and starboard sides.

Porter's most difficult task was to rebuild the warship so that her ends and the eaves of her casement would be submerged. Compared with this delicate engineering task, the job of fitting the *Virginia* with an immense iron ram was easy.

Williamson, who was responsible for the necessary machinery, revised the original plans several times. He made enough improvements in the engines and the propeller to boost the speed of the enormously heavy warship to three knots per hour, which was one-fourth her top speed while operating as a wooden frigate.

Mallory and his three chief subordinates were subjected to constant ridicule. After the vessel surprised its critics by proving to be usable, Porter wrote: "I received but little encouragement from any one [outside the circle of supervisors] while the Virginia was progressing. Hundreds—I may say thousands—asserted that she would not float. Some said that she would turn bottom-side up; others said the crew would suffocate; and the most wise said the concussion and report from the guns would deafen the men. Some said she would not steer; and public opinion generally said she would never come out of the dock."

The *Virginia* proved to be clumsy and slow, yet her coat of metal armor was not heavy enough to drop her unprotected wooden bottom as deeply in the water as the planners had designed. As a result, Porter reluctantly dumped two hundred tons of pig iron into the finished warship as ballast, so that her hull would be completely submerged.

Despite obstacles initially considered to be all but insurmountable, work progressed so rapidly that a crew was assigned to the *Virginia* in February 1862. Capt. Franklin Buchanan, the flag officer, selected as his second in command Lt. Catesby ap R. Jones. Thirty-two officers and aides and more than three hundred seamen were then assigned to a warship like none other the world had ever seen. Buchanan was to test the vessel's machinery and handling during a trial run on March 8. Instead, he put the workmen ashore and, without authorization, took on the Union squadron blockading Hampton Roads, Virginia.

Soon the 1,708-ton USS *Cumberland* settled toward the bottom after having become the target of the metal beak, or ram, of the Confederate vessel. Officers aboard the USS *Congress* tried to turn their vessel and escape, but the mighty guns of the *Virginia* made this impossible. Soon the 1,829-ton Federal warship was disabled and in flames. A third Federal vessel, the *Minnesota,* grounded trying to

THE SOLDIER IN OUR CIVIL WAR

Aboard the CSS *Virginia* (left), members of her crew cheered as the USS *Congress* went to the bottom.

escape. The *Virginia* then retired for the night. Buchanan, who had been wounded by shore fire as he tried to render assistance to the Union sailors in the water, relinquished command of the vessel to Jones.

The Confederate ironclad project was no secret in the North. In July 1861 a special session of the U.S. Congress approved a bill setting aside $1.5 million for the design and construction of one or more ironclads. On August 7 officials of the Department of the Navy announced that they would welcome the submission of plans.

Swedish-born inventor John Ericcson, who had built numerous marine engines and a high-speed locomotive, complied with what he called "an iron-clad battery." Initially rebuffed, he won a contract on September 15 with the stipulation that he could spend no more than $275,000 and must have his craft in the water within one hundred days. He did not quite meet his deadline, but when his *Monitor* slid into the water at New York on January 30, 1862, Federal officials felt that they had no other choice than to accept it with fear and caution.

While the *Virginia* set out on her first cruise, the *Monitor* was being towed toward Hampton Roads as fast as tugs could pull her. Her chief novelty was an immense two-gun turret that could fire in any direction.

The arrival of the Federal vessel the day after the *Virginia* first put to sea led to the epochal battle of March 9, 1862. The two ironclads of different design pounded one another for hours during a contest that naval experts regarded as the day naval warfare was changed for all time. Both were damaged, but neither was beyond repair. Their battle was deemed a draw; however, the *Virginia* never threatened the Federal fleet again.

When the Union army under Maj. Gen. George B. McClellan forced the Confederates to abandon Norfolk, the *Virginia* was torched a second time. A few months later the *Monitor* was transferred to North Carolina, under tow by the USS *Rhode Island*. Ericcson's craft foundered during a gale, ending the career of the second American-built ironclad warship.

Ironically, the designers of the two vessels had tenuous connections to the raging conflicts—Swedish-born John Ericcson did not emigrate to America until he was thirty-six years old. Stephen Mallory's southern roots were shallow, too. Born on the island of Trinidad, the son of a Connecticut civil engineer and an Irish woman, the Confederate secretary of the navy spent most of his childhood at Key West, Florida, where he married Angela Moreno, who was identified in early records as "a Spanish woman from Pensacola." The contributions of these two extraordinary men extended far beyond the national conflict and revolutionized international naval warfare.

7

David Dixon Porter

The Black Terror

DAVID D. PORTER, ONCE a junior crewman on a Mexican warship and briefly a prisoner of the Spanish, joined the U.S. Navy at the age of sixteen. Already a veteran seaman, he fretted because promotions were so slow in coming and considered resigning from the service. He was not only ambitious, he was highly intelligent and inquisitive—always eager to learn something new.

Early in 1863 Porter made a discovery that other officers of the Mississippi Squadron had overlooked. When a small Federal vessel ran the gauntlet at Vicksburg, he noticed that several Rebel guns seemed to burst while firing at her.

Porter pondered this matter for several weeks before arriving at a novel idea. By inducing the Confederates on the high bluffs of the river to fire frequently, he might disable enough of their guns to make an attack upon Vicksburg possible.

Deliberately exposing an expensive vessel to fire likely to sink her would bring a reprimand, if not a court of inquiry. Therefore, Porter sketched a dummy warship. Carpenters among his crew who went to work upon the fake gunboat were skeptical; some of them grumbled at having to waste so much time and energy.

Born in Pennsylvania in 1813, Porter belonged to a distinguished military family. His father, David, had won distinction as a diplomat as well as a naval captain. His cousin, Fitz John Porter, was a brigadier general, and his adoptive brother, David G. Farragut, was a rear admiral.

Late in 1862 Porter had been promoted to commodore and given command of the Mississippi Squadron. He was under no delusions; his vessels would be expected to help master Vicksburg, Mississippi. This heavily fortified river city was the greatest impediment to Union control of the Mississippi River and the heartland of the Confederacy.

It was to induce Rebel gunners to fire so zealously that their guns might explode that Porter set his best artisans to work upon a craft unlike any other. Ens. E. Cort Williams of Ohio was present when the new "craft" was unveiled and said that delighted sailors named her *The Black Terror.* He later noted that he failed to "learn what her own officers and crew called her, for officers and crew she had none."

Porter described the construction of his special vessel: "An old coal barge, picked up in the river, was the foundation to build on. It was built of old boards, in twelve hours, with pork barrels on top of each other for smoke stacks, and two old canoes for quarter boats. Her furnaces was built of mud, and only intended to make black smoke, and not steam."

Williams, who burst into laughter when he first saw the dummy ironclad, wrote his own description:

> She was a most creditable and altogether formidable looking vessel, quite able, in appearance at least, to successfully cope with [the warship] Indianola. Instantly named The Black Terror, she sat low in the water and had a square case-mated gun room on her bow. Built of old boards on her bow, sides of this room were at deep angle. Well back on her quarters, she had the semblance of wheel-houses. All looked invulnerable, thanks to a fresh coat of coal-tar. An immense quaker gun [a piece of fake artillery] protruded from the open port on her bow, making her look a veritable monster.

Federal and Confederate records agree upon one aspect of Porter's vessel: Her maiden voyage down the Mississippi River was the only time she was in motion.

The Confederates did not catch a glimpse of the novel craft until she was ready to be launched, however. Porter saw to it that she lay

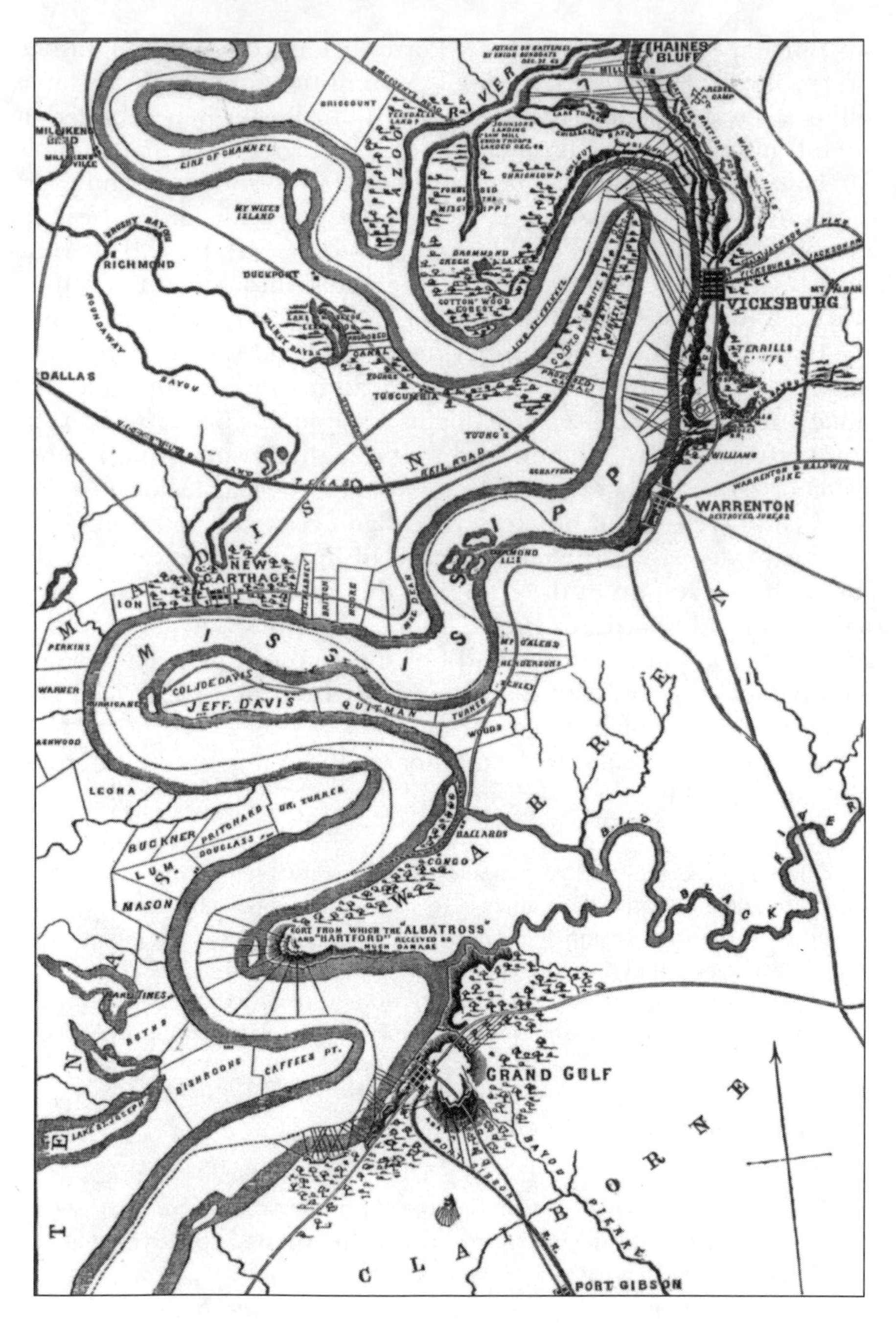

Few major rivers were as twisted and contorted as was the Mississippi for much of its length.

David D. Porter applied the concept of Quaker guns made of logs to his massive fake gunboat.

behind a screen of tall trees while waiting to play a central role in the drama he had planned.

After dark on February 26, 1863, *The Black Terror* was towed into the Mississippi River. Damp oakum in her pork barrels was set afire so that great clouds of smoke erupted. With the skull-and-crossbones flag of a pirate dangling at her fore, the ship carried the Stars and Stripes aft.

According to Ensign Williams, she was at first carried slowly by the current but gradually picked up speed that caused her to "bear down on the upper batteries" at Vicksburg. Sentries soon caught sight of the smoke-belching vessel, but it was too dark for them to realize she was a dummy. Williams wrote:

> They soon saw and challenged her with a shot. Deigning no reply, she stood steadily on her course, as if challenging them to do their worst, and seemingly they accepted the challenge, and the ball opened. The concentrated fire of all the batteries was directed at her; the ball became a picnic; and soon the picnic reached the proportions of a circus with a menagerie attachment. Still no reply from the "Terror;" but, with all the speed that her mud furnaces and a five-knot current could give, she moved proudly on with majestic dignity, apparently uninjured by the storm of shot and shell that followed her course.

According to the designer of the fake gunboat, "Never did the batteries of Vicksburg open with such a din; the earth fairly trembled and the shot flew thick around the devoted craft."

At first light Federal soldiers and sailors lined the west bank of the river, straining to follow the course of Porter's creation. Scores of them "added to the din of cannon fire by their cheers and laughter," said Williams. Soon an eddy in the river caused *The Black Terror* to swirl toward a sandbank; she grounded on it and quickly burned to the water's edge.

There is no reliable evidence that a single Confederate gun burst while firing at the converted coal barge whose only weapon was a painted log, called a Quaker gun. Porter's scheme seemed to have failed, despite the imagination and work that went into it.

Yet the brief cruise of the dummy gunboat revealed that during the darkness Rebel gunners were prone to fire recklessly and in haste. In spite of the hail of iron that was aimed at *The Black Terror,* the clumsy and slow-moving craft managed to get past Vicksburg.

If his fake warship could elude fatal damage, Porter reasoned, genuine gunboats could do the same thing. Hence he arranged to run his entire flotilla downriver in conjunction with troop movements by Ulysses S. Grant. As a result, Grant was soon able to ferry his army across the Mississippi to attack Vicksburg from the east, the only direction from which the city appeared to be vulnerable.

Grant's takeover of the most important Confederate position on the Mississippi River on July 4, 1863, coincided with the conclusion of the battle of Gettysburg. Because fatalities in Pennsylvania were on an unparalleled scale and because Robert E. Lee's vaunted Army of Northern Virginia was defeated there, the Federal victory at Vicksburg did not get the attention it deserved. Measured by any standard, however, the capture of Vicksburg was among the most important successes of Union military forces.

For his role in the capture of Vicksburg, the man who first went to sea at age ten was made a rear admiral. Late in 1864 he took command of the North Atlantic Blockading Squadron, and in that capacity helped to close the last important port of the Confederacy—Wilmington, North Carolina.

Many accounts insist that Porter received the rarely given Thanks of Congress three times; others contend that he received the coveted commendation four times. Whatever the case, at war's end the architect of *The Black Terror* who sent her on her only voyage was among the most highly decorated commanders on land and sea.

8

Sam Upham

Paper Bullets

According to his friends, "Sam Upham had the time of his life getting together a circular about his doings." Widely distributed in Union territory, the printed piece consisted largely of excerpts from newspaper editorials. One of the most prominent silently shouted: "Rebeldom Highly Indignant—Yankee Trick."

The longest of what the Philadelphia merchant called "testimonials" purportedly came from the Confederate capital. It said that a detective of the Southern Treasury Department had gone to the editor of the *Richmond Dispatch* with a warning for its readership:

> The last and grossest piece of Yankee scoundrelism is an infernal means to discredit the currency of Southern Confederacy. It consists of well executed counterfeits of our five dollar Confederate notes, struck off in Philadelphia, where the news-boys are selling them at five cents a piece. This note is well calculated to deceive, and in nearly every particular is a fac-simile of the original. We caution persons receiving this money to be exceedingly careful, as there is no means of knowing to what extent they have been circulated.

Although he was not the first to distribute bogus Confederate currency, Upham became widely known for his achievements. After having had an immense number of phony bills printed and initially sold as souvenirs, he began referring to his merchandise as "paper bullets." He knew that his counterfeits were contributing to inflation in Rebel territory and were undermining confidence in an already shaky medium of exchange.

When the Confederate States of America was formed, an immediate need was to provide its citizens with legal tender. U.S. currency was redeemable in specie (gold or silver), but the Confederacy had only a small supply of precious metals, much of which had been seized from the New Orleans branch of the U.S. Mint.

Following the precedent of the Continental Congress during the Revolution, the Confederates printed their own paper money, not backed by gold. They made arrangements with the New Orleans branch of the New York–based American Bank Note Company to produce a batch of five-dollar bills.

Engravers created a set of eye-catching steel plates to print about one million dollars' worth of currency on high-quality paper especially made for the purpose. This early Confederate currency had an aesthetic appeal—one bill was two-toned black and red—and persons handling it were impressed with its feel. To the average citizen, however, such interest-bearing notes had a major drawback: They could not be redeemed in precious metal until after peace was concluded between the United States and the Confederate States.

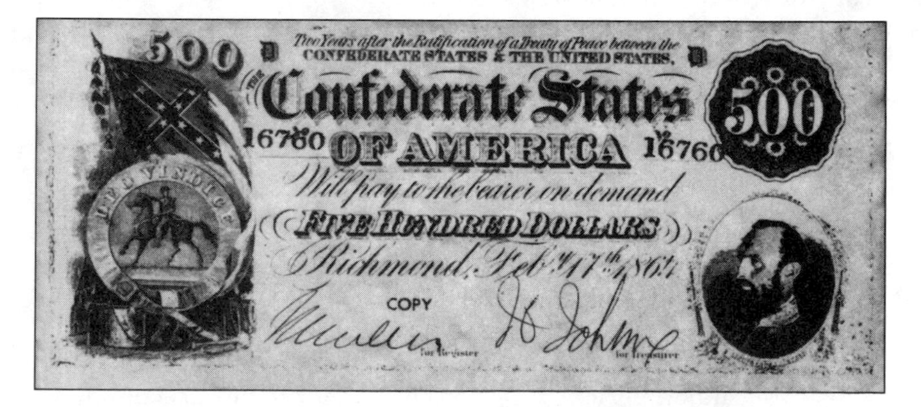

Considered worthless for more than a century, genuine Confederate currency is now a collector's item, regardless of its denomination.

Gold and silver were comparatively abundant in Union territory. In 1861 the U.S. government began issuing paper money to finance the war effort, and in 1862 the notes were no longer redeemable in coin but were only promises by the United States to pay. The backs of these notes were printed in green ink, which led to their being called "greenbacks." As they were not secured by precious metal, their value fluctuated, sometimes to as little as thirty-five cents in coin for each dollar. The National Bank Acts of 1863 and 1864 set up a system to rectify this by limiting the number of bank notes that were issued, sometimes causing shortages of paper money. Although U.S. Treasury practices have since changed, the popular name for paper bills remains.

Meanwhile, the Confederacy's monetary problems grew. Secretary of the Treasury Christopher G. Memminger did his best to stabilize the Southern economy and its treasury, but he was hampered by the states' rights philosophy that was basic to the Southern cause. Gov. Joe E. Brown of Georgia was one of several state leaders who said it was necessary for him to issue his own fractional currency—paper money with face value less than one dollar. Barring use of this expedient, Brown insisted, "commerce would dry up, because some of our

BATTLES AND LEADERS

Confederate Secretary of the Treasury Christopher G. Memminger.

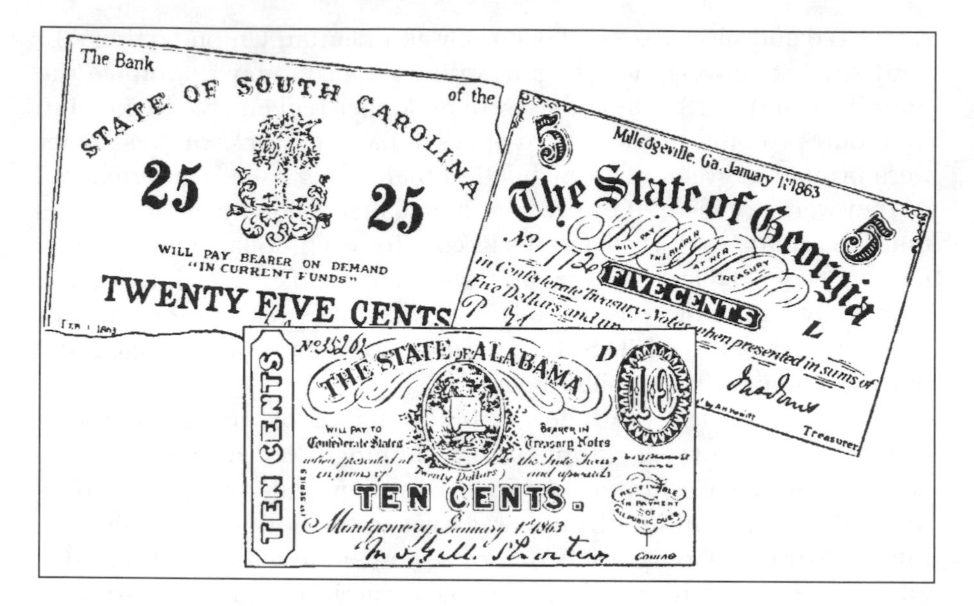

Every state in the Confederacy issued its own variety of fractional currencies worth as little as five cents.

most ardent patriots are hoarding metal coins." The problem continued to grow, and desperate merchants even printed and distributed their own notes with face values of one, two, three, five, and ten cents.

When Gen. William Tecumseh Sherman took command of occupied Memphis in 1862, a delegation of citizens informed him that businesses were in dire need of local scrip (currency backed only by the city's promises). According to H. Seymour Hall, later a Union brevet brigadier general, after giving his full attention to the matter, Sherman said his answer would appear in the public press. "The next morning," said Hall, "the Appeal and Avalanche published a letter from the general that recited the request made to him before giving them a stinging rebuke for their treason and for having declared cotton to be king." Sherman's public letter concluded: "I cannot authorize you to issue city scrip, but to relieve the pressure complained of, I suggest that, inasmuch as you have declared cotton to be king, you tie up cotton in 5-, 10-, 15-, 25-, and 50-cent packages, and pass that around for change."

Banknotes issued from Richmond, whether for one dollar or one thousand dollars, were suspect from the beginning of their existence. As early as June 1862 at faraway Santa Fe, Col. J. M. Chivington found that citizens "will not touch the Confederate scrip."

Widespread distrust of Southern currency led Confederate Gen. Braxton Bragg to issue a special order at Lexington, Kentucky, in the fall of 1862. He commanded all persons within his military district to "take the paper currency of the Confederate States at its par value in all transactions, public or private." Disobedience of the order would be treated as a military offense, Bragg warned, "and punished accordingly."

About a year later the grand jury of Twiggs County, Georgia, requested the court to compile a "Black Roll" listing people who refused to accept Confederate bills as payment. Such a roll, the jurors believed, would serve to have "names of malcontents officially handed down to posterity, and their ultimate reward insured."

Clearly, Confederate currency was in serious trouble long before Sam Upham conceived the notion of mass producing counterfeit bills. He later said he got the idea when an issue of the *Philadelphia Daily Inquirer* sold out quickly because it carried a reproduction of the five-dollar Confederate bill on its front page.

Upham acquired the plate used by the newspaper, took it to a nearby print shop, and ordered three thousand copies of the Confederate banknote. He'd pay for them only if they were "printed on French letter paper," he stipulated. Offered for sale as souvenirs at one cent each or fifty cents per hundred, he found plenty of eager buyers.

The Vermont native next secured a plate from New York used to display another Confederate note in a newspaper. By this time the market for his counterfeits was much larger than his city. A supply of his first two issues was transported into Tennessee where the bogus currency was sold to citizens of the Volunteer State at thirty and forty cents on the dollar.

No one knows how many print shops in border-state towns had already turned out counterfeit Confederate currency. Smugglers knew that genuine bills were of such poor quality that ordinary folk would not spot the difference when handed a worthless piece of paper.

Back home in Philadelphia, Upham enlarged his counterfeiting operation to include Confederate stamps and expanded his line of merchandise every time he received an original that could be copied. In at least one instance, he purchased a bill from a stranger and then copied it and sold the copies, not knowing that the original was counterfeit.

If his records are accurate, Upham eventually distributed more than 1.5 million counterfeit bills of many denominations. Long before that total was reached, however, agents of the U.S. government questioned him in his general store. Initially frightened, he protested that he had done nothing illegal and "was only trying to hurt the Rebels a little bit in their pocket books." Soon he realized that he had nothing to fear. His visitors simply wanted to learn where he got his originals, who did his printing, and how his counterfeits were distributed. Those who bought Upham's counterfeits said that "the quality of his work improved soon after he thought his shop would be closed by officials from another city."

One undocumented story suggested that U.S. Secretary of War Edwin M. Stanton supplied the enterprising counterfeiter with banknote paper. According to the tale, many Southern blockade-runners had English-made paper among their cargo for use by the Confederate treasury. Some of it was said to have been "nicely finished, with bold CSA watermarks." As the Northern blockade grew increasingly effective, more and more banknote paper was captured. When Upham received it, some purchasers noted that the quality of his "little souvenirs" showed dramatic improvement.

With inflation already soaring in the South, vast quantities of fake currency in circulation boosted prices even higher. John Wilkinson, a blockade-runner who was still evading capture in 1864, complained of the prices he had to pay when he reached Rebel ports: "A quarter of lamb sold for $100, a pound of tea for $500." By January 1865 flour cost one thousand dollars per barrel in Richmond.

How much damage was done to the Rebel cause by Sam Upham and others like him who operated on a smaller scale, no one knows. It must have been substantial, since Jefferson Davis spoke out forcefully about its evils. Bogus bills were disseminated, he said, by enemies who were totally without scruples and operating with the knowledge of the Federal government.

Certainly, the "prince" of the Civil War counterfeiters knew that soldiers on both sides had to have paper cartridges to fire their handguns. To some, it seemed that Sam's special variety of "paper bullets" was among the most effective missiles aimed at the South.

When the war ended, Lincoln came to Richmond. During his brief triumphal visit, he tucked a souvenir into his wallet. Unlike tens of thousands of counterfeits, it was a genuine Confederate bill, and it was worthless except as a memento of the war. Sam Upham would have been gratified had he known in the spring of 1865 that when the president died, the only currency in his pocket could have been one of his counterfeits.

9

Robert Smalls

Captain for a Day

F. G. RAVENEL'S REPORT on May 13, 1862, to Confederate Brig. Gen. R. S. Ripley is a most unusual war document.

> GENERAL: I have to report that the steamer Planter was stolen from the Southern Wharf [at Charleston] between 3 and 3.30 o'clock this morning and taken to the enemy's fleet, where she was visible till late in the forenoon. By telegram from [the] Stono [region] this afternoon it is reported that she has gone south. The Planter is a high-pressure light-draught boat, drawing ordinary not more than 3½ to four feet [of water], and has been employed in Confederate service in the transportation of ordnance, &c., to and from the various posts in the harbor and other localities in the neighborhood. She passed Fort Sumter at 4.15 o'clock [this morning], and was reported by the sentinel on duty to the officer of the day. She was supposed to be the guard-boat and [was] allowed to pass without interruption.
>
> F. G. Ravenel
> Aide-de-Camp

During the Civil War no other vessel was seized by the South or the North as was the *Planter*. The boat's experienced pilot had planned

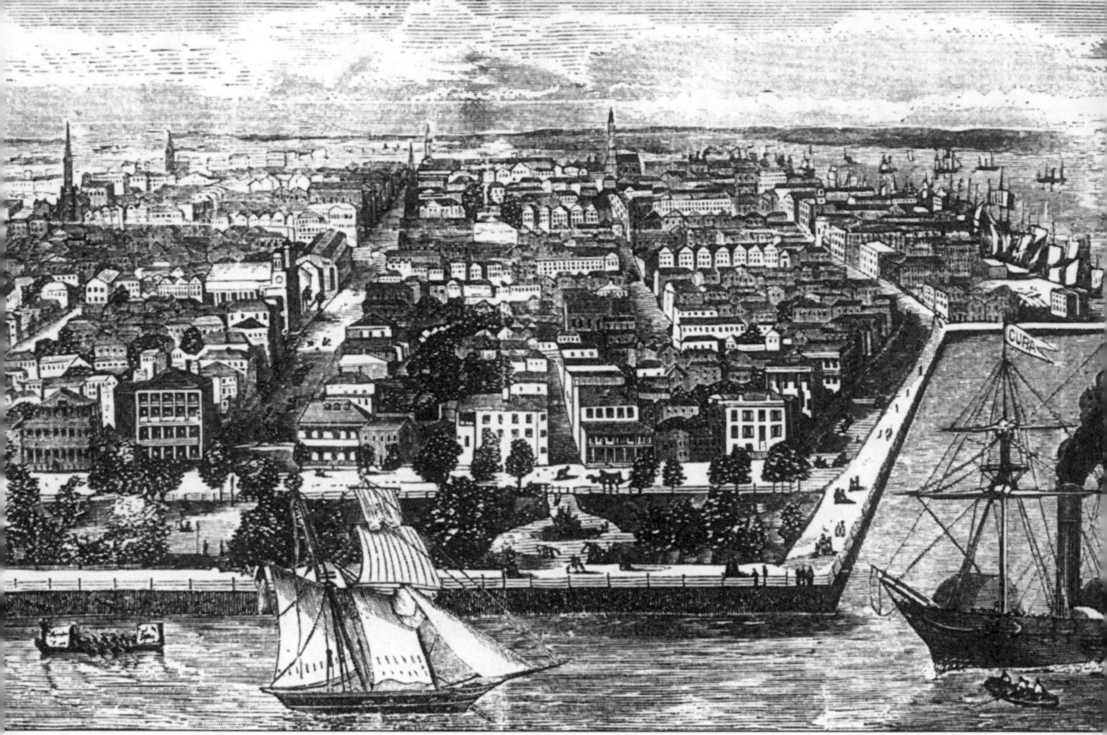

LIBRARY OF CONGRESS

Charleston's busy waterfront as depicted by an English artist a decade before the outbreak of war.

for months before he had the opportunity to become captain of the vessel for one day. He was aware that he could not take the little ship from Charleston Harbor without being challenged. When hailed, he would have to identify himself as C. J. Relyea, the real captain, and announce a bogus destination. That meant he must learn to speak like the master of the *Planter* before venturing on what he hoped would be a short one-way voyage.

Having been reared in Beaufort, South Carolina, the mastermind of this unique scheme appeared and talked like every slave of the Palmetto State's Low County. African natives who worked the plantations of the Low Country often spoke with a pronounced Gullah or Geechee accent. It would take vigilance and diligence for one of these slaves to speak without betraying himself. No one knows how long Robert Smalls practiced, but once he was confident that he could sound like Relyea, he began perfecting other aspects of his daring plan.

Although small, the steamer *Planter* was received by Federal naval forces with jubilation.

Although his education was limited, Smalls could write well enough to keep a log of his short but momentous journey. According to the *New York Tribune,* he prepared a list of the people on board when the boilers of the *Planter* were fired at about 3:00 A.M. It took the small messenger steamer a full hour to reach Confederate-held Fort Sumter, where his risk of detection was great. Arriving at the Federal blockading squadron, Smalls inserted an exultant entry in the log: "We give three cheers for the Union flag."

From Port Royal Harbor at Beaufort, Samuel F. Du Pont reported the daring voyage of the Confederate vessel to Washington just one day after Ravenel informed Ripley what had happened. After escaping from Charleston Harbor, the *Planter* was consigned to the care of Comdr. E. G. Parrott of the USS *Augusta.* Both the warship and "the late rebel steamer" reached the huge Federally held harbor some time during the night of May 13.

Du Pont was then serving as flag officer in command of the South Atlantic Blockading Squadron. He described the vessel brought to him as being "an armed dispatch and transportation steamer attached to the [Confederate] engineer department at Charleston." Having served on warships for thirty-seven years, Du Pont gave U.S. Secretary of the Navy Gideon Welles his appraisal of the Smalls exploit: "The bringing out of this steamer, under all the circumstances, would have done credit to anyone. At 4 in the morning, in the absence of the captain, who was on shore, she left her wharf close to the [Confederate] Government office and headquarters, with palmetto and Confederate flag flying, passed the successive forts, saluting as usual by blowing her steam whistle. After getting beyond the range of the last [enemy] gun she quickly hauled down the rebel flags and hoisted a white one."

Du Pont's lengthy report included a summary of the guns mounted on the *Planter* at the time of her escape: "The armament of the steamer is a 32-pounder, on pivot, and a fine 24-pounder howitzer. She had, besides, on her deck four other guns, one 7-inch rifle, which were to be taken the morning of the escape to the new fort on the middle ground. One of the four belonged to Fort Sumter, and had

SOUTH CAROLINA STATE LIBRARY

Congressman Robert Smalls, later collector of customs at his hometown.

HARPER'S WEEKLY

"Black codes" against which Smalls waged an unsuccessful fight permitted thugs to confront would-be black voters who dared to go to the polls.

been struck, in the rebel attack on that fort, on the muzzle." In addition to the naval prize, Du Pont inherited sixteen escaping slaves: eight men, five women, and three children.

In his appraisal of Smalls, Du Pont said that he "is superior to any [slave] who has yet come into the lines. . . . His information has been most interesting, and portions of it of the utmost importance." It was his plan, wrote Du Pont, to "continue to employ Robert as a pilot on board the *Planter* for the inland waters, with which he appears to be very familiar."

Soon the now-free black man was sent up the St. Johns River and the *Planter,* as part of the U.S. Navy, was attached to the U.S. gunboat *Seneca.* Built of wood and rated at only three hundred tons, the former Confederate vessel, which was powered by wood-burning twin engines, was 147 feet long and 30 feet wide. Since she was capable of operating in less than four feet of water, she was expected to be extremely useful on the rivers of South Carolina.

One bit of information imparted by Smalls had to do with what had earlier been a substantial Confederate base. To the surprise of the men in blue at Port Royal, the escapee assured them that the Rebels had abandoned their works at Stono, a spot just south of Charleston regarded as strategically important in 1862. When Du Pont dispatched some vessels to make a reconnaissance, it was found that the information was accurate. Since Stono no longer posed a threat, the Federal gunboats *Unadilla, Pembina,* and *Ottawa* crossed the bar there in open daylight, and Du Pont gleefully reported on May 22 that this maneuver caused the Confederates in Charleston to think that "their time had come."

Since the *Planter* was treated as a war prize seized from the enemy, Congress allocated payment to Smalls for having delivered this "contraband of war." Compared with ironclad warships, the ship was tiny, yet its symbolic importance was significant. Widely publicized in the North, the story of "Captain Smalls" and his exploit helped to influence public opinion in favor of using former slaves as Union soldiers. When the official records of Civil War naval actions were published, a photograph of the tiny vessel that was built for the cotton trade rated an entire page.

Smalls fared well. Custom and prejudice made it difficult for an African American to enter the U.S. Navy. His exploit, however, enabled him to serve quietly but effectively as a pilot on the *Planter,* and he became the ship's captain in 1863.

After Appomattox, Smalls took off his Federal uniform and joined the South Carolina militia. During the dozen years he served in that organization, he rose to the rank of major general.

Three years after hostilities ended, Smalls won election as a delegate to a statewide convention called to frame a new constitution. Soon he became a member of the legislature of the Palmetto State. After one term, he moved to the state senate and from that post became the first southern black to go to the U.S. House of Representatives.

Except for a two-year interval, the former slave remained in Congress from 1875 to 1887. Then he was appointed collector of customs in his hometown of Beaufort. He held the post for more than a decade and won the respect of his fellow citizens of both races. As a member of the state's 1895 Constitutional Convention, he fought to abolish "black codes" that served effectively to bar members of his race from voting.

10

Brutus de Villeroi

Underwater Warfare

A NEWCOMER TO PHILADELPHIA with a French accent liked to hang out along the waterfront. To casual acquaintances he let it be known that he was close to perfecting "an entirely new kind of craft," but he refused to be more specific.

Once the Civil War started, Brutus de Villeroi was viewed with increasing suspicion. It was easily possible, reasoned some authorities, that he was an agent of South Carolina or Louisiana, since both seceded states included substantial numbers of French-speaking citizens.

Arrested on May 17, 1861, de Villeroi proved obstinate, but naval officers learned where his handiwork lay and examined it. Comdr. Henry K. Hoff reported to his superiors, "The Frenchman has built an underwater craft whose external form resembles a whale." Work was so far along that Hoff estimated it would take only a few days to submit the weird craft to experimental tests, if that should prove to be desirable.

Upon his release, the inventor sent messages to Abraham Lincoln and to the secretary of the navy, Gideon Welles. He wanted to sell his novel craft, he said, "in the hope that it could help bring a speedy end to present hostilities."

After examining the specifications submitted by the inventor, Commo. Joseph Smith was keenly interested but pronounced the tiny vessel lying at a Philadelphia dock to be "entirely too small to be of military use." At his urging, the U.S. Navy entered into a contract with Martin Thomas, who agreed to build a substantially larger version of "the de Villeroi craft," and he hired the inventor as superintendent of construction.

Several delays brought the project into the new year, unfinished. Commodore Smith was by this time convinced that the novel vessel—now called the *Alligator*—could be of tremendous importance. He knew that Confederates soon would finish converting the *Merrimack* (now rechristened the CSS *Virginia*) into a formidable ironclad, and he doubted that any conventional craft could stand up against her.

On May 1, 1862, nearly a year after de Villeroi's arrest, the enlarged and modified version of his invention was launched. Two weeks later the builder turned over the operation of the *Alligator* to Samuel Eakin of the U.S. Navy. Reluctant to proceed "with undue speed," Eakin did not formally agree to accept the oar-propelled underwater vessel until mid-June.

By that time, the thought was that the *Alligator* might serve to annoy the James River defenses. All such notions were dismissed by Flag Off. Louis M. Goldsborough, who commanded the North Atlantic Blockading Squadron. In the opinion of this longtime U.S. Navy officer, the *Alligator* was "a next to useless matter." It didn't take an experimental run to demonstrate that he was right concerning a possible role for the craft in rivers. The *Alligator* could not function in water less than eight feet deep, and in late June many Virginia rivers were too shallow for her.

By August most of the naval officers involved in the project were calling it a failure. Its backers, however, were unwilling to give up so easily, so they replaced the oars of the craft with a screw propeller. After months of work, the conversion was completed, and the *Alligator* was demonstrated for President Lincoln late in the winter of 1863.

At this time Commo. Samuel Francis Du Pont, commander of the South Atlantic Blockading Squadron, was vexed at the stubbornness of the Fort Sumter defenders and the ease with which Confederate craft maneuvered in and out of Charleston Harbor. He decided to test the Frenchman's invention and ordered the *Alligator* to be towed to Charleston. No one knows how she would have performed in combat, because the first U.S. submarine went to the bottom during a gale in the spring of 1863.

Meanwhile, in New Orleans, a pair of entrepreneurs heard about de Villeroi's whale-shaped contrivance and set out to build a similar craft. Since James R. McClintock and Baxter Watson were well educated, they may have known that David Bushnell had tried to put an underwater vessel to work against the British during the American Revolution. His *Turtle* was never pitted against a warship, but the idea of operating a vessel below the surface of the water was still intriguing.

Since Jefferson Davis had issued a proclamation offering letters of marque, at least four other citizens of New Orleans became interested in the enterprise: H. J. Levy, Horace L. Hunley, John K. Scott, and Robin Barron. Early in 1862 their efforts produced the tiny *Pioneer,* successfully tested in Lake Pontchartrain. The fall of New Orleans in April 1862 led them to scuttle their vessel to prevent its capture. Years later, the wreck was discovered and pulled to the surface.

Having secured a license to raid Yankee shipping, the builders of the *Pioneer* did not give up. They went to Mobile, where Maj. Gen. Dabney H. Maury, commander of the port, suggested that they employ the machine shops of Park and Lyons. There artisans, aided by two young Confederate officers, built the South's second submarine, unofficially referred to as *Pioneer II.* In February 1863 foul weather and rough seas caused it to sink without loss of life as it was being towed to attack the Federal fleet.

Some of those persons involved in the project gave up, but Hunley vowed that he would spend his entire fortune working for its success. He supervised the cutting of an iron boiler in two, welding the longitudinal sections together, and providing the contraption with water tanks that could be filled or emptied to lower or to raise what had become a prototype submarine.

It was impossible to use a coal-fired boiler to provide motive power, so the Mobile builders devised a complex system of oars that required constant work by seven muscular men. When they pulled together smoothly, the *H. L. Hunley* achieved the surprising speed of four miles an hour in smooth water.

Another inventor, whose name was not recorded, came up with an idea for using explosives. A strong hemp rope about two hundred feet long was securely attached to the rear end of the *Hunley.* At the far end of the rope, a copper cylinder that held nearly one hundred pounds of powder constituted what was called a "torpedo," which was rigged to explode on contact.

This cross section depicts a member of the *Hunley's* crew ready to move the craft by applying himself to the hand-turned propeller.

"Take our vessel below the surface, move invisibly to the side of a Yankee vessel, then dive under it," the operators were told. "Once past the target, come near the surface again and proceed so that the floating torpedo will be pulled against the side of the warship and blow a huge hole in it."

An initial test in the Mobile River gave Hunley and a few associates great satisfaction, and the vessel was shipped by rail to Charleston. There Maj. Gen. P. G. T. Beauregard, commander of the city's defenses, ordered a trial run. It ended in disaster with all onboard killed except Alabama-born Lt. John Payne.

Hunley was discouraged until he and a handful of other enthusiasts heard of a tiny Confederate vessel that had headed for the enemy with a torpedo attached to a long spar that protruded from its nose. The not-quite-submerged craft commanded by Lt. William J. Glassel rammed the powerful USS *New Ironsides.* The resulting explosion of the torpedo put the warship out of commission for many weeks.

Payne, who had already recruited a second crew for his tiny submarine, persuaded his associates to drop the idea of the towed

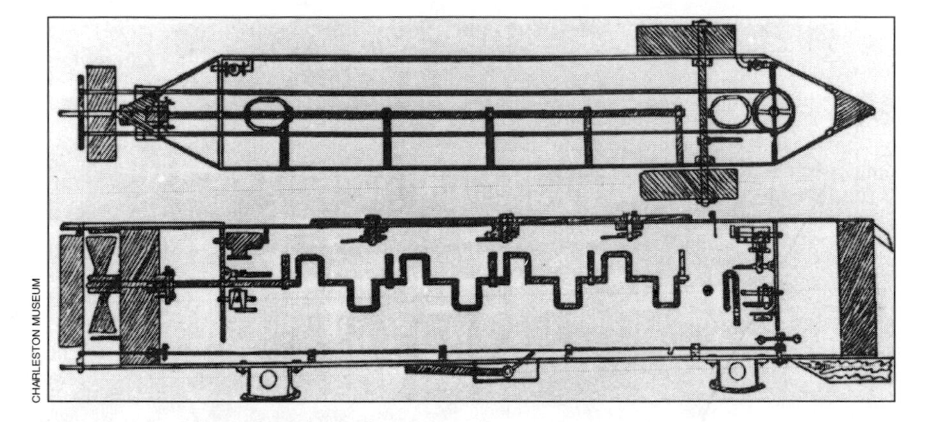

CHARLESTON MUSEUM

This schematic drawing shows the apparatus (lower) by which the crew served to propel the *Hunley*.

torpedo and place a torpedo-equipped spar on the bow of the craft so it could ram the enemy. This modification boosted the chance that the *Hunley* could attack a larger enemy vessel, but it did not increase its seaworthiness. At least seven men are thought to have drowned when the submarine was tested again.

Beauregard regretted having approved the experimental use of the novel craft, but he was persuaded by Hunley to give her one more chance. This time the investor-builder himself headed a crew of men who had gone underwater at Mobile and lived to tell of their exploit. On the morning of October 15 this trial run led to the death of Hunley and every member of his crew.

Since no heirs of the builder claimed his handiwork, the Confederates treated it as property of their government. When word of the most recent tragedy linked with the *Hunley* reached Mobile, one of the engineers who had helped build it hurried to Charleston where Beauregard had delegated use of the submarine to Brig. Gen. Thomas Jordan. Although the *Hunley* had been built as an underwater craft, Jordan suggested that it could be operated on the surface, where there would be a better chance of success without endangering the lives of the crew.

Beauregard seems to have consented to the adaptation, but with reservations. He permitted men from the crew of the CSS *Indian Chief* to sign a sheet that was headed: "New Volunteers for Duty aboard the *Hunley*." Probably without Beauregard's knowledge, the new crew decided to revert to the builder's plans and operate their vessel at an

P. G. T. Beauregard led the 1861 assault upon Fort Sumter and later commanded the defensive forces during much of the siege of Charleston.

NATIONAL ARCHIVES

underwater level sufficiently low to make it virtually invisible to the enemy. A series of successful new test runs revealed that the craft could stay underwater for more than two hours without suffocating its crew.

By mid-February 1864 a tempting Federal target had been selected. On the night of February 17, the *Hunley* set out for the twelve-hundred-ton USS *Housatonic*, a heavily armed screw-steamer only a few weeks old. Lookouts on her deck spotted "a strange looking shadow" moving through the moonlit waters and signaled for action. Her big guns could not be depressed enough to fire at the suspicious object, so riflemen began peppering it.

A slight lurch on the part of the Federal warship sent it rapidly in the direction of the *Hunley*, and the two vessels collided. The torpedo at the end of the spar that stretched ahead of the *Hunley* exploded, and the immense warship went to the bottom in a matter of minutes. Most of the crew of the *Housatonic* were rescued, but two officers and three men were lost; however, all those aboard the *Hunley* were lost, either from the explosion or from being unable to disengage from the warship as it sank. Naval history had been made nevertheless—the first sinking of an enemy ship by a submarine.

Part 3

Bizarre as a Byzantine Novel

HARPER'S WEEKLY

Southern children mock an abolitionist in this engraving by cartoonist Thomas Nast.

11

William H. Seward

One Way to Avoid Civil War

ON APRIL 1, 1861, Abraham Lincoln was handed one of the most unusual documents ever to reach the desk of the chief executive. Written by his secretary of state, William H. Seward, it detailed a scheme to avert civil war. By any standard it was an astonishing memorandum.

The secretary began, "We are at the end of a month's administration and yet without a policy either domestic or foreign." Had that scathing critique come from an eastern newspaper editor who bitterly opposed the election of the man from Springfield, it would have been ignored. Since it represented the considered judgment of the man who was nationally known as "Mr. Republican," the statement was confrontational. In effect, Seward was challenging the president to one-on-one combat to determine the course of the nation.

Seward's beginnings were almost as plain as those of Lincoln. He was born in a small village of no more than a dozen households in midstate New York. His childhood in Orange County was an uneventful prelude to his years at Union College. After his graduation in 1820 he read law and opened a practice in Auburn.

Since the twenty-two-year-old attorney had about as good an education as could then be obtained in the country, he was poles apart from Lincoln. Born near Hodgenville, Kentucky, eight years later than Seward,

Lincoln was a product of the western frontier. Reared in Illinois and Indiana by his stepmother, his formal education was limited to brief periods in what he always called "blab schools." Lincoln borrowed a few books from an attorney, plowed laboriously through them, and won his license to practice law thirteen years later than did Seward.

Both men were politically ambitious. Running as a Whig, Lincoln won a seat in the Illinois legislature two years before becoming a lawyer. He sat in this body for four terms, then spent a single term in the U.S. House of Representatives.

Debates with Stephen A. Douglas during the 1856 senatorial campaign attracted national attention. In ninety-four Illinois counties, members of the fledgling Republican Party endorsed Lincoln, but he never had a realistic chance of defeating Douglas. According to the *Chicago Tribune,* Lincoln's loss was partly due to "outside intermeddling," with *New York Tribune* editor Horace Greeley being the chief meddler. Though he had not held an elected office for a dozen years, in 1860 Illinois political leaders made Lincoln their "favorite son" presidential nominee.

Seward was elected to the New York senate four years before Lincoln went to the Illinois legislature. It took him just eight years to build a political base strong enough to facilitate his election as New York's first Whig governor. After holding this post for two terms, the native of Florida, New York, became a founding father of the Republican Party and was elected to the U.S. Senate, which had also been Lincoln's aspiration. During his second term in Washington, Seward became a confidential adviser to President James Buchanan and a nationally renowned orator.

The views of the two men on the most divisive issue of the day—slavery—were almost as different as their backgrounds. Lincoln opposed the westward extension of slavery but was willing to tolerate it where it existed. He favored gradual abolition, with compensation to slave owners and the overseas colonization of freed slaves. Seward, however, was a fiery abolitionist who wanted immediate action of the most drastic kind.

Seward's views concerning slavery caused him to form conspicuous political alliances, one of which was with Sen. John Sherman of Ohio, whose younger brother was destined to lead the March to the Sea in 1864. During the Thirty-fifth Congress (1857–59), James L. Orr of South Carolina was Speaker of the House. Sherman, widely

LIBRARY OF CONGRESS

John Sherman, brother of William Tecumseh, stumped his political toe upon a little book written by a native of North Carolina.

expected to succeed him, was nosed out by William Pennington of New Jersey.

Sherman's defeat stemmed largely from what lawmakers from the slave states called "an unholy alliance." That terminology came from Sherman's open praise of ideas put into print by North Carolina native Hinton R. Helper.

After wandering through several states and visiting California, Helper set out to analyze the economic plight of the South and its residents. It stemmed largely, he concluded, from the fact that white laborers faced economic competition from slaves. This internal tension in the South, said Helper, was rapidly approaching the boiling point.

In 1857 Helper published his analysis of the southern dilemma in a volume he called *The Impending Crisis in the South and How to Meet It.* Issued in an attempt to better the condition of whites at the bottom of the economic ladder, it blasted slavery as the cause of their plight.

Small as it was, the Helper volume created a national uproar. Many people in the Cotton Belt castigated the author and burned copies of his book. Numerous people in the North, John Sherman being prominent on the list, praised Helper and had portions of his book reprinted and distributed. Republicans are believed to have circulated at least one hundred thousand copies of excerpts from the North Carolina book during the campaign of 1860.

After *The Impending Crisis* became a topic of heated argument, Seward made an October 1858 address at Rochester and in it referred to what he called "the irrepressible conflict." To abolitionists, who were strong in most of the northeastern states, Seward's phrase was just the kind of ammunition they wanted. To slaveholders and their constituents in the Deep South, his words constituted a direct threat. To vast numbers of people who did not live in the slave states but were not proponents of abolition, talk of an irrepressible conflict was frightening.

At least four months before Seward's speech, Lincoln's correspondence indicates that he had his eye on the White House. To Charles L. Wilson he wrote on June 1, 1858, that he believed "Govr. Seward, too, feels about [Douglas] as Greeley does." That is, he regarded Seward as backing Douglas in the Illinois contest for the U.S. Senate.

Having made himself clear concerning his opinion of a man he did not know, Lincoln wrote: "As to myself, let me pledge you my word that neither I, nor any friend of mine so far as I know, has been setting stake against Gov. Seward. No combination has been made *with* me, or *proposed* to me, in relation to the next Presidential candidate." With the next election scheduled for November 1860, it was taken for granted that Seward would seek the Republican nomination.

Late in the winter of 1860, Lincoln took a speech-making swing through key cities far from the frontier. Although newspaper reporters made fun of his appearance and his western twang, he could hold listeners spellbound for long periods. At the renowned Cooper Union in New York City, he evoked great enthusiasm by his arguments in favor of limiting slavery in the western territories. A few days later in both Hartford and New Haven, he voiced the Helper theme by saying that slavery's "effect on free labor makes it what Seward has been so roundly abused for calling, an irrepressible conflict."

Although his diction was poor by eastern standards, Lincoln was both a master of words and a skilled politician. His comment concerning Seward seemed on the surface to be a commendation of the presidential aspirant, yet it succeeded in introducing the inflammatory term "irrepressible conflict."

There is no reason to believe that Lincoln's platform references to Seward had any impact upon the Republican Convention of 1860.

An informal poll of the delegates headed to Chicago revealed that a majority believed that the New Yorker would be nominated. On the first ballot, he came close to winning the prize, and his backers were jubilant that victory was in sight.

Astute tactics by Lincoln's campaign manager and the fears aroused by Seward's outspoken expectation of an irrepressible conflict changed the outcome of the Republican conclave. The victory of the comparatively obscure man from Springfield stemmed partly from the fact that many delegates felt they knew too much about the senator from New York.

Seward's bruises began to hurt a bit less when he was named secretary of state in the Lincoln cabinet. He and his adherents took it for granted that the frontiersman whom many of them considered to be a buffoon would be chief executive in name only. Many expected that the secretary of state would be making the key decisions for the new administration.

No one was more confident than Seward that this was to be his role. In cabinet meetings as well as in discussions and correspondence, he

Chicago erected a special building, The Wigwam, for the Republican National Convention of 1860.

repeatedly expressed firm convictions he knew to be at variance with those of his chief. To him, it was obvious that the myriad demands and baffling perplexities of the Executive Mansion would quickly prove too much for a man whose experience didn't seem to be adequate.

Seward's emphasis upon the fact that sectional conflict was inevitable did not prevent the New Yorker from trying to stave off civil war. He let South Carolina and Confederate emissaries know that he preferred to evacuate Fort Sumter and expected Lincoln to take this course. Hence it was natural for him to concoct a scheme that he believed would avert national attention from hot spots in South Carolina and Florida.

Seward's proposals aimed at "easing tension by means of diversion" were spelled out in the second half of his April 1 recommendations to Lincoln: "I would demand explanations from *Spain* and France, categorically, at once. I would seek explanations from Great Britain and Russia, and send agents into *Canada, Mexico,* and Central America, to rouse a vigorous continental *spirit of independence* on this continent against European intervention. And if satisfactory explanations are not received from Spain and France, Would convene Congress and declare war against them." Whatever foreign policy should be adopted, he urged, someone must "pursue and direct it incessantly. Either the President must do it himself . . . or devolve it on some member of his Cabinet."

Seward's proposal was based on his knowledge that Spanish colonists in San Domingo had staged a minirevolt a few weeks earlier. In response to their actions, Spain had dispatched the ship *Blanc* from Havana with troops to assist the rebels in annexing the country to Spain.

A president "without a policy, either domestic or foreign," totally without experience in dealing with the leaders of other nations, was obviously unfit to take the momentous course suggested by his secretary of state. Little imagination is needed to deduce which cabinet member Seward had in mind to "pursue and direct" U.S. foreign policy calculated to bring about war with Spain and France and reduce domestic sectional tensions.

On the day he received Seward's recommendations, Lincoln drafted a reply. Since this letter was found years later in the president's papers rather than in Seward's, it seems never to have been sent. Skilled as he was in personal relationships, Lincoln may have gathered his thoughts by putting them on paper and then given Seward an oral summary.

The president's written reply to the question of who would implement policies, once adopted, was unequivocal: "If this must be done," he concluded, "*I* must do it." Seward's proposal to shift national attention to a war with Spain and France must have been regarded by Lincoln as ridiculous. His letter to Seward did not so much as mention the matter. No other Civil War scheme conceived by a top-level Washington leader was rejected so quickly and so silently as was the idea of averting civil war by fomenting a foreign war.

12

Thomas J. Jackson

A Big Catch of Fish

NEWS THAT THE VIRGINIA Convention had adopted an ordinance of secession on April 17, 1861, reached Harpers Ferry the following day. Situated on what is now the border between Virginia and West Virginia, the isolated hamlet was the site of the largest Federal arsenal in the South.

West Point–graduate Roger Jones Jr. was in charge of the token forty-five-man garrison stationed there. Believing correctly that Secessionists would immediately set out to seize the arsenal and armory, Jones knew any resistance he could offer would be futile. Hence he ordered his men to torch all buildings and supplies that might have military value and then withdrew to the closest Federal installation, which was at Carlisle Barracks, Pennsylvania. U.S. Secretary of War Simon Cameron was later informed that the appraised value of the arsenal's 1,670 acres of land with its dams, canals, hydraulic machinery, forges, machine shops, tools, and weapons was $1,470,513.

Meanwhile, Virginia Gov. John Letcher was reorganizing his state's military units. He called to Richmond a relatively obscure professor at the Virginia Military Institute who was a major in the state militia. Thomas J. Jackson was made a colonel of Confederate

LOSSING'S PICTORIAL FIELD BOOK OF THE CIVIL WAR

John Letcher probably conceived the idea of seizing Harpers Ferry from Federal forces.

infantry and sent to Harpers Ferry, whose strategic communications and transportation importance the governor recognized.

Jackson's inventory revealed how badly Jones's plans had gone awry. Thousands of muskets were undamaged; others needed only minor repair to become useful. By mid-May, the man called "Old Jack" by his students was shipping repaired artillery to strategic Southern sites as fast as he could access railway cars via the branch railroad that ran to Winchester, thirty miles away.

Col. Kenton Harper and Capt. John D. Imboden, subordinate to Jackson, helped to plan and execute the cleanup of the arsenal by the Fifth Virginia Infantry. Chests were mounted on farm wagons to form improvised caissons because the Federals had burned most of the ammunition carts. Much machinery was repaired on the spot, while other pieces were shipped to Richmond. Once the armory had been emptied of all ordnance, Old Jack turned his attention to the Baltimore and Ohio Railroad that was Washington's principal connection with the West.

Extremely reticent about revealing his plans even to his top officers, Jackson muttered something about a fishing expedition. This puzzled his aides, as everyone knew Jackson was not one to indulge in recreational activity.

Nevertheless, following orders from his commander, Harper led a force to a temporary camp at Martinsburg, Virginia, nearly ten miles west of Harpers Ferry. At the same time, Imboden established a post at Point of Rocks, Maryland, about the same distance to the east.

Thomas J. Jackson, here shown as a major general, had not yet become known as "Stonewall."

W. G. JACKMAN ENGRAVING

Twenty miles of the Baltimore and Ohio Railroad, double track the entire distance, connected the two points.

At Harpers Ferry the railroad spanned the Potomac River by covered bridge. Having dipped south into Virginia, it recrossed the river near Martinsburg and continued to Cumberland, Maryland. According to Jackson's best estimate, about 120 miles of the line lay within his command.

The tight-lipped Southern commander spent hours in the field, riding a horse left behind when the Federals fled. Never attended by more than one aide and often alone, Jackson studied the hills, the river, its bridges, and the rail lines—especially the rail lines.

Many years earlier, a two-hundred-mile canal had been the primary transportation system in the region, but the railroad had long since supplanted the waterway as the main shipping vehicle. The Baltimore and Ohio track was Washington's sole link with the West. By mid-May 1861 it was one of the busiest lines on the continent. Trainloads of coal and farm produce moved eastward in a constant stream, and empty cars flowed west.

While Jackson was becoming familiar with the topography of his command, he perfected a plan he occasionally called "a fishing expedition." He respectfully requested that the railroad schedule its trains so that his men could sleep without disturbance. The railroad

A remote mountain village in western Virginia, Harpers Ferry was the site of a huge arsenal.

president, John W. Garrett, complied with the request, and Baltimore and Ohio traffic was restructured to pass through Harpers Ferry during daylight hours only.

After a few days Jackson claimed that several men in the machine shops had been injured when they were distracted by the commotion of the trains passing through town. He would schedule a daily break between 11:00 A.M. and 1:00 P.M. if Garrett would arrange for the trains to run only during this period. Eastbound trains could perhaps use one track and westbound trains the other so the flow of traffic would not be disturbed.

Well aware that something unusual was in the offing, Imboden later wrote that when the new schedule went into effect, the twenty or so miles of double track on each side of Harpers Ferry were the liveliest railroad in America for two hours every day.

Continuing his account of the events that then took place, Imboden remembered: "One night, as soon as the schedule was working at its best, Jackson sent me an order to take a force across the river to the Maryland side the next day at 11 o'clock, and to let all westbound trains pass until 12 o'clock. We were ordered to obstruct the road at 12 o'clock so that it would take several days to repair it. He ordered the reverse at Martinsburg. Thus he trapped all trains going east and west between these points."

Jackson left no account of what took place, and evidence from Federal sources is scanty. Yet a May 14 telegram from Brig. Gen. Edward Shriver to Benjamin F. Butler, his commanding officer, reported: "Danger is apprehended at the Monocacy Bridge to-night. An engine and cars were seized at Harper's Ferry at 2 o'clock to-day. All connections west are cut off since 8 o'clock to-night. We are guarding the wire as far as Our forces enable us. Please send us immediate relief." Butler referred the matter to Lt. Gen. Winfield Scott, asking for instructions.

Imboden's summary fails to explain that "obstruction of the road" involved blasting huge boulders onto the track at Point of Rocks. With the section of double track also firmly closed at Martinsburg, Jackson sorted through his catch before a Federal response could be planned and executed.

When he found that he had snared 64 locomotives and 378 boxcars, he realized that he had more than he could handle. Unless he acted swiftly and decisively, Federal units were likely to charge into the region to recapture the all-important rolling stock.

Jackson immediately sent a few locomotives and cars thirty-two miles to Winchester by the Winchester and Harpers Ferry Railroad. From Winchester, forty-horse teams pulled the locomotives overland to the Manassas Gap Railroad at Strasburg.

He could not spare the men needed to move the rolling stock; thus several units were put to work destroying bridges in an effort to isolate the captured locomotives and cars. They pulled down or blew up nearly two dozen structures, including the 837-foot span at Harpers Ferry.

On June 2 Jackson's zealous men set fifty twenty-ton coal cars on fire and pushed them into a gorge to collapse a heavy railroad bridge over the Opequon River. Weeks later a writer for the *National Intelligencer* found that the red-hot coals had melted and misshappened many axles and wheels: "We counted the line of locomotives (41 or 42 in all) red and blistered with the heat. The destruction is fearful to contemplate." The Federals had no chance to get their hands on even one of the trains snared by Jackson, but some locomotives and cars remained where their crews had abandoned them.

Two weeks later, on June 17, Jackson was promoted to brigadier general as part of Gen. Joseph E. Johnston's army. The next month, at First Manassas, he acquired the nickname "Stonewall" by which he is known to history.

Three days after his promotion, Jackson visited Martinsburg and was surprised to find the rail yard crammed with his "catch." Believing it would be impossible to move them into secure Confederate territory, he ordered them destroyed. Sledgehammers, fire, and explosives damaged but did not demolish all the rolling stock. Jackson therefore sent to Richmond for experienced railroaders. They dismantled the locomotives and cars, salvaged the best parts, and devoted months to hauling a dozen locomotives and nearly one hundred cars overland to Strasburg. Put back into service on the Manassas Gap line, much of this salvaged equipment served the South throughout the war. Jackson's haul constituted the largest capture of locomotives and boxcars during the Civil War and added immeasurably to the vitality of the transportation-challenged Confederacy.

13

Josiah Tattnall

Refit and Fight!

In 1861 a Confederate naval captain prophesied that before the Southern navy could contend successfully with the Northern fleets "my bones will be white in the grave." The Confederate navy to which he referred was the product of an agricultural nation locked in an industrialized war. With no seafaring tradition and few shipyards, the newly declared nation had to hustle to fight at sea and to maintain a lifeline of goods from abroad.

Two men who contributed immeasurably to the Southern naval cause were Caleb Huse and James Bullock. A West Point graduate and professor of chemistry, mineralogy, and geology, Huse had taught at the U.S. Military Academy and was at the University of Alabama when the war broke out. He then accepted a commission as a captain in the Confederate service. His background in science, administration, and ordnance made him a wise choice to be the army's European purchasing agent.

After serving as a lieutenant in the prewar U.S. Navy, Bullock had resigned to become captain of a commercial vessel carrying mail for the U.S. government. He offered his services to the Confederate navy, and naval secretary Stephen Mallory appointed him a civilian agent to secure ships and equipment from abroad. Both Huse and Bullock are credited with prolonging the war through their creative abilities to fulfill their missions.

Huse was authorized to purchase "any and all available munitions of war" at the best possible price. He acted so swiftly that critics said he failed to make perfunctory inspections before signing contracts. Wondering if he was lining his own pockets at Confederate expense, Richmond authorities sent Maj. C. J. McRae to audit his records.

It took McRae only a few days to decide that everything done by Huse was legitimate. One reason for the lavish expenditures was the soaring price of weapons and munitions, he learned. Soon the two men became close friends who worked together on purchasing expeditions for much of the summer of 1861. When Bulloch joined them, the Confederacy had a formidable team at work far from the scenes of battle.

By spending lavishly the Confederates managed to get a contract that required the London Armory Company to sell everything it produced to them. Soon so much war materiel was accumulated that a huge supply remained after the steamer *Bermuda* had taken a partial load to a Confederate port. When Bulloch learned of the fast-growing store of arms in dockside warehouses, he suggested that they purchase a vessel that could be loaded to the gunwales with the weapons and supplies waiting for shipment.

Searching England's busiest ports, Bulloch discovered a freighter just three months old. Especially built to sail between Scotland and the Orkney Islands, she was a screw-driven steamer that was schooner-rigged with two masts. For a price never disclosed, Liverpool merchant C. A. Byrne purchased the *Fingal* through the firm of Frazer, Trenholm and Company and took possession in Greenock, Scotland.

By the time the transaction was completed, Union representatives in England had become suspicious. They knew the Liverpool-based mercantile firm was a subsidiary of a Charleston, South Carolina, shipping and banking company. From London, the U.S. consul, F. H. Morse, informed the secretary of state, William H. Seward, of the purchase, surmising that the *Fingal* "is in reality a Confederate ship, and will change her papers on arriving at some port in the rebel States and then turn pirate."

On October 11 Morse sent to Washington a description of the vessel, accompanied by a drawing. Copies of the sketch were transmitted to the South Atlantic Blockading Squadron, commanded by Flag Off. Samuel F. Du Pont. Captains of all ships in the squadron were alerted to the approach of a British-built vessel with "a round stern, the bust of a man for a head, one deck and a poop, 186 feet long and 25 feet wide with 12.9 feet depth of hold."

Long before the warships of the Federal blockade received these details, both Bulloch and Anderson had decided to return home on the *Fingal.* Bulloch took precautions, because he feared that British authorities might be persuaded to prevent the ship from sailing. Later he learned that some Union agents, posing as longshoremen, had pried open boxes of rifles to find out what firm had made them.

Since the *Fingal* was to sail under the British flag, it was necessary to employ a captain who held a board of trade certificate. To dispel suspicion, Bulloch instructed the captain to hire British sailors rather than men of all nationalities who hung around ports hoping for work. As an additional precaution, the ship initially sailed to Wales rather than toward the open sea.

Edward Brennan, working for or with the U.S. consul in London, on October 10 reported the *Fingal*'s 8:00 A.M. departure: "She drew at starting 10 feet forward and 11 feet aft; she is very deep laden. Her mate informed me she is bound to Cuba and other West India ports."

After a stormy three-day voyage from Greenock to Holyhead, off the coast of Wales, Bulloch and Anderson boarded the Confederate ship. Still flying the British flag, the *Fingal* reached Saint George, Bermuda, well before dawn on November 2. At first light a government boat approached bringing a health officer. Fearing the arriving vessel was a disease-carrying slaver, he refused to come aboard to inspect but consented to have water and provisions sent from the town.

From the beginning, Bulloch had planned to take his ship to Savannah; now he began to wonder if they would be able to slip through the blockade. He was glad to learn that the CSS *Nashville* had just anchored in the same port to take on coal, also badly needed by the would-be blockade-runner. During the coaling operations Bulloch managed to contact Lt. Robert B. Pegram of the *Nashville.*

To Bullock's surprise, he learned that the Confederate warship had been expecting his arrival for more than twenty-four hours. In fact, she was in these waters to provide coastal pilots for the last and most dangerous leg of the *Fingal*'s voyage.

Soon after her coal bunkers had been filled early on the morning of November 6, the *Fingal* headed toward Savannah. As planned, the vessel neared her destination in darkness. With every light extinguished, the blockade-runner moved slowly toward the Wilmington River, from which the pilot expected to enter Wassaw Sound.

LESLIE'S ILLUSTRATED HISTORY OF THE CIVIL WAR

One of the military engineers who helped to design and build Fort Pulaski was Capt. Robert E. Lee.

As they approached the coast, a lookout shouted a warning; a range beacon at Tybee had disappeared and the lighthouse appeared to be empty. The ship's master had to wonder. Had the Federals captured Fort Pulaski? Were they waiting for the *Fingal* to come within range before opening fire?

There was no turning back now, however. The ship moved over the bar into the Savannah River in the misty light of early morning. Simultaneously, the Confederate flag was raised to the top of the mainmast. Peering at Pulaski through his glass, Bulloch smiled for the first time in hours. Instead of gunfire from the fort, his rising emblem had prompted the gunners to wave enthusiastically. Moving rapidly up the river, the heavily laden ship had nothing further to do except to anchor and unload at Savannah.

Reports concerning the cargo of the first voyage made by the first blockade-runner owned by the Confederate government vary. Describing her safe arrival to Gen. William Tecumseh Sherman, Du Pont relied on papers provided by the secretary of the navy, Gideon Welles. According to what he termed "a complete invoice," Du Pont believed the cargo to be valued at $48,336. That total, he said, represented

11,340 rifles, 400,000 cartridges, 24,000 pounds of powder, and 500,000 percussion caps.

An October 12 dispatch from Greenock, Scotland, indicated a cargo made up of 410 boxes, 73 barrels, 236 casks, 1,091 cases, and 1 trunk. In addition to the items enumerated by Du Pont, the list recorded the *Fingal* as carrying 500 sabers, 4 pieces of ordnance, 1.5 tons of lead shot, 7 tons of shells, 230 swords, 9,982 yards of blanket material, and assorted apothecaries' wares.

A report by Bulloch indicated that his purchase and voyage brought to the Confederacy 14,000 Enfield rifles, 1,000 short rifles with cutlass bayonets, 500 revolvers with ammunition, 3,000 cavalry sabers, two 4.5-inch muzzle-loading rifled guns with plenty of shot and shell, two 2.5-inch steel-rifled guns, 400 barrels of cannon powder, 1 million ball cartridges, 2 million percussion caps, and "a large quantity of made-up clothing for seamen."

Regardless of the precise inventory, the authorities in Richmond rejoiced at the arrival of the priceless war materiel. They did not know that the *Fingal*'s cargo would be the largest single shipment of weapons ever to reach them from abroad.

For the moment the question was how next to use the British-built vessel. With the blockade growing tighter by the day, it appeared unwise to send her back to England immediately. Heavily loaded with cotton, she was moored in the Wilmington River so that she could slip through the network of warships as soon as the authorities thought Yankee vigilance was relaxed.

Before the Confederates could make that determination, Washington had enacted a bizarre scheme. In mid-November a fleet of twenty-five old whaling vessels assembled at New Bedford and New London in Massachusetts. Each was heavily loaded with stone—a total of 8,376 tons—designed to block all channels leading to Savannah. On December 5 Comdr. J. S. Missroon reported that seventeen of these ships were on station, ready to be sunk.

By the time his message was received, Du Pont had a different order en route to him. Missroon was at liberty to sink any vessel at Tybee he wished; the others were to be towed to Port Royal, South Carolina. Confusion then set in on the Federal fleet because by December 21 most of the hulks had been sunk off Charleston trying to render that vital port unusable. Thus the stone fleet, did not block the *Fingal* at Savannah, but the vessel was still unable to move because of the tight blockade.

Josiah Tattnall, right, with Franklin Buchanan—first commander of the CSS *Virginia.*

Now entered Josiah Tattnall in the continuing saga of the *Fingal.* Tattnall was the Confederate naval captain charged with defending the Georgia–South Carolina coast. The *Fingal* had eluded British authorities, evaded Federal warships, and avoided sunken whalers loaded with stone. "Refit her and fight!" Tattnall urged, and his proposal was approved. Renamed the CSS *Atlanta,* the blockade-runner was converted into a man-of-war.

Teams of workmen cut the ship down so that when she was fully loaded her deck rode only two feet above the waves. Four-inch railroad iron was rolled into plates two inches thick and fastened over her hull to a depth of about three feet below the water line.

Four Brooke rifles were mounted in the casemate, and six-inch guns went into both midship ports. Installation of two seven-inch pivot guns at the bow and stern gave the British-built vessel sufficient firepower to stand up to lightly armed Federal warships. As a final step, her bow received a heavy cast-iron ram that ended in a "torpedo spar," or heavy explosive designed to go off upon contact.

By the time refitting was completed, only the USS *Cimmerone* was maintaining the blockade of Savannah. When Du Pont learned in May that the *Atlanta* was nearly ready to try to break the blockade, the

The CSS *Atlanta,* formerly the blockade-runner *Fingal.*

Federal flag officer acted quickly. At his command, both the *Weehawken* and the *Nahant* joined the *Cimmarone* off Savannah.

On June 17, 1862, the *Atlanta* headed downriver on her first voyage. The Confederates were as confident that day as the Federals had been on the morning of First Manassas. Many of them crowded aboard two steamers following the new warship to see her do her deadly work.

When a lookout spotted the Confederate vessel, Capt. John Rodgers of the *Weehawken* signaled, "Beat to quarters." Within a quarter-hour his powerful ship slipped her cable and steamed directly toward the entrance to the Savannah River. In her wake followed the *Nahant,* handicapped by lack of a pilot familiar with the waters.

Just before 5:00 P.M. the *Atlanta* fired the first shot, which went considerably wide of its target. No response came from the *Weehawken,* whose master had earlier said he wanted to engage the enemy at close quarters. When he was within one-sixth of a mile from his quarry, Rodgers gave the order, and fire belched from both his fifteen-inch and his eleven-inch guns.

Four of the first five shots fired from the Federal vessel hit their target. From his post Rodgers saw the first shell penetrate the armor of the Confederate ship, causing forty or more men to fall to the deck wounded or semiconscious from the concussion. His second shot hit, but the damage could not be ascertained. Not so with his third, which shattered the pilothouse and left both pilots dazed.

When the fourth shot from the Federal warship also hit squarely, the *Atlanta*'s Confederate flag was hauled down and replaced with a white banner. After less than fifteen minutes against an enemy vessel with firepower many times her own, the *Atlanta* was surrendered.

On her first voyage, the *Fingal* made history and extended the military life of the Confederacy. Once she became a warship, however, the first sortie lasted less than a day and ended in humiliating defeat. During the entire naval struggle, no other ship built in England had double lives so memorable as those of the *Fingal/Atlanta.*

14

Gustavus V. Fox

A Fleet of Stone

No one ever publicly claimed credit for hatching one of the strangest schemes implemented during the war. Signs point toward Gustavus V. Fox, but if he actually was the instigator of the idea to send hundreds of tons of strange cargo to the South, he kept quiet about his role. The bizarre plan surfaced during the summer of 1861, around the time that Abraham Lincoln created the post of assistant secretary of the navy and named Fox to fill it.

The written evidence begins August 3 when Secretary of the Navy Gideon Welles dispatched a confidential order to Comdr. H. S. Stellwagen, informing him: "Sir: You have been selected for the very important duty of closing certain Southern ports by sinking vessels loaded with stone. Communicate with the Department in person before sailing, and give all practicable dispatch to this duty."

Immediately after having signed this order, Welles sent word to Flag Off. Silas H. Stringham of the Atlantic Blockading Squadron that Stellwagen "has been detailed to procure the necessary vessels for the stoppage of the ports of North Carolina." It took Stringham only three days to challenge Washington's strategy. Writing from the USS *Minnesota,* then anchored in Hampton Roads, he reported that he had talked with "several captains of vessels who have been in North

LOSSING'S PICTORIAL FIELD BOOK OF THE CIVIL WAR

Lincoln protégé Gustavus V. Fox, assistant secretary of the navy.

Carolina." These men were unanimously opposed to the sailing of what became known as the stone fleet. Stringham stated, "They all pronounce it as of little use; because of the light and shifting nature of the sand [at Cape Hatteras] a new inlet would soon open."

Disregarding that negative verdict from a veteran seaman, landlubber Welles issued instructions to Stringham on September 3. "The Department," he wrote, "in pursuance of the plan matured under its directions has to request you to block Oregon and Loggerhead inlets [by sinking in them old whaling vessels loaded with stone.]"

On September 13 Fox instructed Stringham to assume personal direction of the operation. The new assistant secretary of the navy wrote that Stellwagen, who evidently had been voicing strong objections, "will have no further connection with affairs in the vicinity referred to."

The fulfillment of the project was relegated by Stringham to Flag Off. Louis M. Goldsborough, who promptly requested that twenty-five men of the Coast Guard be assigned "five of the vessels loaded with stone, to be sunk at certain points along the coast of North Carolina, by direction from Washington."

Late in September officials in the Navy Department prepared a list of the vessels that had been purchased to be loaded with stone and sunk at Cape Hatteras, of which six were identified as manned by a captain and two crew members: *J. Alexander, E. Goldsborough, Alvarado, South Wind, Somerfield,* and *Friendship.* Sixteen other vessels, presumably smaller ones, had been purchased and added to the strange fleet that departed from Hampton Roads in September.

Bad news reached Washington less than two weeks later. Six armed Confederate steamers had been seen several times in the waters to which the stone fleet was headed. To make matters worse, according to Stellwagen, "no first rate pilot could be procured" for the difficult task of proceeding twenty-five miles through "shoal water that is channel crooked." At the time he dispatched this explanation for his failure to obey orders, he said that there were only eight "schooners with stone ballast" still afloat at Hatteras. Of these, he considered five to be "pretty good."

Soon Jacob Westervelt, pilot of the USS *Ceres,* was consulted concerning obstructing Ocracoke Inlet. Writing on October 15, he did not mince words: "I consider any attempt to block it up by sinking vessels would only be of short duration, not lasting thirty days, before there would be as good navigation as ever."

Lt. R. B. Lowry of the steam tug *Underwriter* voiced the same verdict on October 29 and went into greater detail in explaining why it would be futile to sink the stone-laden vessels as ordered: "No earthly power can stop the rush of [waters inside the inlet] to their destination—the ocean." Bottom sands seemed almost to be "alive and creeping." Hence, he warned, movements of currents would make it impossible to block any of the North Carolina inlets "for any practicable end or definite results."

Regardless of what these men or others might think, orders were orders. By November 15 three schooners "chained together, bow and stern" had been sunk in nine feet of water. Lt. T. S. Phelps of the coast survey steamer *Corwin* exulted that New and Loggerhead Inlets were "effectually closed." Like the brass in Washington, Phelps failed to realize the power of rushing water; within weeks new channels were cut. As a result, the sunken hulks had no effect whatever upon Southern navigation.

Fox was no man to be deterred by what he considered a minor impediment to a master plan. If the waters of North Carolina were not suitable for the use of granite-laden hulks to abet the blockading squadrons, he reasoned, add to the survivors of the stone fleet to form a new and larger one and send it to Savannah.

Welles, who had been a prewar newspaper publisher, readily assented to the new suggestions. Thus George D. Morgan of New York was instructed on October 17 to work with Richard Chappell of

WHALING MUSEUM

Part of the great stone fleet that sailed from New Bedford, Massachusetts, in November 1861.

New London, Connecticut, and purchase "twenty-five old vessels, of not less than 250 tons each, for the purpose of sinking on the bar at Savannah."

Each vessel of the second stone fleet was to be loaded to capacity with blocks of granite. "Have a pipe and valve fitted under skillful direction, so that after anchoring in position the water can be readily let into the hold [in order to sink each vessel at a designated spot]," he was told. Consulted about the expanded operation, Du Pont told Fox: "Captain Rodgers and myself have conferred very fully upon the subject of sinking obstructions at the entrance of the Savannah River, and we agree that the best point for this operation is the narrow channel above Tybee light [about twenty miles seaward from Savannah]."

The Georgia port was considered to be a vital target because the blockade-runner *Fingal* was known to be there, waiting for a chance to slip past Federal warships. By November 7 the twenty-five vessels intended for Savannah had been purchased, along with twenty more that were destined for Charleston Harbor. The captains of these worn-out vessels were told to rendezvous at Port Royal, South Carolina, and wait for orders.

Du Pont, charged with the execution of what had become a two-pronged operation, proceeded slowly and cautiously. He did not report until December 26. Instead of again consulting Washington, he turned to Brig. Gen. Thomas W. Sherman, who was in command of an expeditionary corps stationed on Hilton Head Island, South Carolina.

Exploration had shown, Du Pont said, that the Savannah River was not the only water route to the city. A second entrance, the Wilmington River, had potential for making the stone fleet useless. Therefore, along with the Savannah River, the Wilmington River must be blocked by sinking "stone ships at the place where it empties into Wassaw Sound."

Sherman, who had sent a reconnaissance into the target area, hesitated. He wrote back that he wanted to know "the positive facts." A careful examination of Wilmington Narrows should be made before taking action. If this showed the point in question to provide easy access to Savannah, "then stop up the Wilmington River," replied Sherman. On the last day of 1861, Du Pont ruefully reported that "the typography of Tybee Island induces me to suspend for the present the sinking of the stone vessels at the mouth of the creek coming into Wassaw Sound."

The third target, Charleston, was a place of symbolic importance because the war had started there. When it began, the stone fleet had been reduced in size by the accidental sinking of some of the vessels that had been barely able to stay afloat for their southward voyage, but sixteen of the strongest members of the fleet eased out of Port Royal and headed for Charleston.

In command was Capt. Charles Henry Davis, who had succeeded in getting a firsthand look at Charleston Harbor. As a result, he had developed a precise plan for sinking his vessels. They would go down, he announced, precisely on the bar of the harbor in indented formation intended to create a material obstruction to the channel without seriously impeding the flow of water.

Davis told Du Pont that the sunken stone-filled hulks would "establish a combination of artificial interruptions and irregularities, resembling on a small scale those of Hell Gate or Holmes' Hole, and producing, like them, eddies, whirlpools, and countercurrents, such as to render the navigation of an otherwise difficult channel hazardous and uncertain."

Maj. Thomas M. Wagner of the South Carolina artillery, who was in command at Fort Sumter, noticed a dramatic increase in the size of what he thought was the Federal blockading squadron on the afternoon of December 18. He was puzzled that "the majority of vessels appeared to be old whaling and trading vessels," and he wondered why they were accompanying warships.

According to Wagner, two days later fifteen vessels "were placed in line more or less direct across the main ship channel." He watched

FRANK LESLIE'S ILLUSTRATED NEWSPAPER

Some vessels of the stone fleet that were sunk in Charleston.

as these ships were "stripped, dismasted, and sunk" at intervals of about one hundred feet along a thirty-five-hundred-foot path that seemed completely to occupy the channel. Within a week, Wagner could no longer see even a trace of these members of the stone fleet.

On January 20 he watched as fourteen smaller vessels—barks and brigs—were towed into position and sunk. Aboard the warships *Augusta* and *Pocahontas,* Comdr. E. G. Parrott and Lt. George B. Balch framed separate but almost identical reports on January 26. According to both of them, the operation had been successfully completed after a delay caused by a heavy northeastern gale. Both Federal officers were confident that their goal had been accomplished; blockade-runners would no longer be able to slip in and out of Charleston Harbor past the warships.

Du Pont was elated. Reporting to Washington, he said of Charleston that "the obstruction there is complete." Though surviving documents do not indicate that Secretary of State William H. Seward was involved in planning the Charleston expedition, Welles transmitted a summary of it to him on February 17. The birthplace of armed rebellion, he said, had been the recipient of about thirty-six sunken vessels. Each carried a full load, with the smallest bearing about 250 tons of stone and the largest carrying fully 400 tons.

A correspondent of the *New York Times,* who sailed from Port Royal to Charleston, filed a lengthy report that ended on a note of exultation: "The work of the expedition is a complete success. If it seemed sometimes a sad one even to us, with what feelings must the people of Charleston have looked on its progress? The fire which swept the streets of half the city was trivial misfortune compared with this final disaster. All access by the main ship channel is effectually closed. The bar is paved with granite, and the harbor a thing of the past."

One of the most elaborate naval schemes of the war seemed to have been wholly successful at Charleston. Mapmakers duly plotted and then marked the site at which approximately twenty-four million pounds of granite had been dumped.

Years afterward, Brig. Gen. Stewart L. Woodford told a group of New York veterans the conclusion of this episode. By the time Woodford was stationed in Charleston toward the end of the war, the military effects of dumping all that granite were nonexistent. Of the mighty Federal effort, Woodford said, "The spring tides swept out the hulks of the stone fleet and broke them up, and soon their great ribs bleached along the shores of Morris and Folly Islands, by their ghostly appearance scaring the poor contrabands and making our horses shy as we rode down the beach by moonlight."

Like Fox and Welles, Woodford knew little about the sea and did not realize that marine worms, or toredos, began to feast upon rotten wood almost as soon as the vessels of the stone fleet went to the bottom at Charleston. Once the old whaling and commercial vessels began to release their heavy cargoes, swift-moving water cut new and deeper channels. Hence the harbor where the war began suffered only a brief interruption in its role as a haven for blockade-runners.

15

A Pennsylvania Miner

The Crater

DOZENS OF MEN AND a few officers knew the name of the man who concocted the deadliest of Civil War schemes, but no one bothered to preserve it in writing. This much is known with certainty: he was a coal miner who had spent years in the tunnels of the upper Schuylkill region of Pennsylvania.

This anonymous but experienced and highly skilled miner may have joined the Forty-eighth Pennsylvania Infantry when it was organized at Harrisburg in September 1861. Or possibly he volunteered later and was assigned to take the place of a member of the Forty-eighth who had fallen in battle.

Members of his outfit fought at Groveton, Chantilly, South Mountain, and Antietam. During the Ambrose E. Burnside expedition to North Carolina in April 1862, the Forty-eighth went to North Carolina. Later it was attached to the Army of the Potomac and the Army of the Ohio, and many members of the regiment reenlisted on December 7, 1863. As a result they were rewarded with a three-month furlough, after which they fought in the Wilderness, at Spotsylvania, North Anna River, Cold Harbor, and Bethesda Church. On June 16 battle-weary veterans found themselves before Petersburg, which Lt. Gen. Ulysses S. Grant had determined to take by siege.

At his City Point headquarters, Grant was interested when he learned of the scheme initially proposed by the unidentified miner. The Pennsylvanian had grown weary of the tedium resulting from sitting day after day only four hundred yards from a Confederate position too strong to storm. Drawing upon his long experience, he suggested that a tunnel be dug and loaded with gunpowder to blow a hole through the Rebel line.

It is surprising that Grant did not dismiss this notion without a second thought. At Vicksburg a similar tunnel scheme under his direction had failed to do its work; however, Grant was willing to try almost anything as his siege was stalemated.

By the time the general gave his approval, work on the elaborate project was under way. Miners in Brig. Gen. Robert B. Potter's division of the Federal Ninth Corps seem to have talked things through before going to the commander of their regiment, Lt. Col. Henry Pleasants, who had been a mining engineer in civilian life.

Pleasants pointed out major obstacles that would have to be overcome but gave fairly enthusiastic support to the scheme. After it was passed by Potter, the plan for the world's longest tunnel was approved by Burnside. Maj. Gen. George G. Meade, who was in command of the sector involved, was less enthusiastic about the plan to plant gunpowder directly beneath a major Confederate position. His subordinates later quoted him as calling the scheme "all clap trap and nonsense." He seems to have been reluctant to pass the notion along to Grant and was clearly surprised when the general approved it.

Work on the tunnel began around June 25, 1864, and soon became an all-demanding task. Pleasants had planned to use only a few dozen men on the job, but he increased the workforce several times. Eventually he complained that he had to use his entire regiment, including noncommissioned officers, to push ahead.

Immense quantities of dirt had to be removed, as the tunnel was about fifty-four inches wide at the bottom and two feet wide at the top. Its five-foot height, however, facilitated the arduous work. Since wheelbarrows were not available, Pleasants bound old cracker boxes with iron hoops pried from pork barrels. Equipped with wheels, these crude devices functioned remarkably well.

Pleas for lumber to support the ever-lengthening underground gallery received no response. In desperation, the workers tore down the remnants of a bridge and salvaged two-by-fours and four-by-fours.

LIBRARY OF CONGRESS

Cracker boxes plus picks (as conceived by an artist) were the chief tools used in digging the tunnel.

A request amounting to a demand seems to have reached the secretary of the army in Washington, but it did not produce a single miner's pick such as the men of the Forty-eighth said they couldn't do without. Challenged to modify army picks, regimental blacksmiths turned out earth-digging implements that users said were "grotesque in appearance, but fully as useful as those employed in coal mines."

Pleasants was immersed in the task of securing these necessities and claimed he could not finish the job without accurate instruments to make triangulations for determining positions. This request also got nowhere, so in desperation he settled for a surveyor's theodolite that was obsolete but functional.

Earth was wheeled out in the cracker-box barrows during darkness; in the morning the tunnel entrance was covered with freshly cut saplings. This precaution seemed unnecessary to some diggers, since the Confederates who were entrenched on the ridge partly occupied by Blanford Cemetery could not possibly see the opening.

When Pleasants, however, announced that work would stop unless his orders were followed to the letter, the soldiers grudgingly hid the entrance of the tunnel every morning after having hauled out the dirt.

When the tunnel was completed around July 23, its main gallery measured a little over 510 feet in length. A lateral gallery 37 feet long had been dug to the right and another 38 feet long to the left. These secondary tunnels lay in roughly semicircular fashion directly beneath the advanced positions of the Confederates.

Regardless of the caution with which the men worked, some of them occasionally dropped a pick or struck a rock when digging. Dim sounds filtered through twenty feet of earth into a salient held by troops under the command of Confederate Maj. Gen. P. G. T. Beauregard. When his subordinates reported what was being heard, he ordered squads to sink holes into the ground in an attempt to locate what was underground. When nothing resulted from these probes, Beauregard stopped them.

Meanwhile, Pleasants had no idea that the enemy had become suspicious, but he faced another major challenge. To continue their

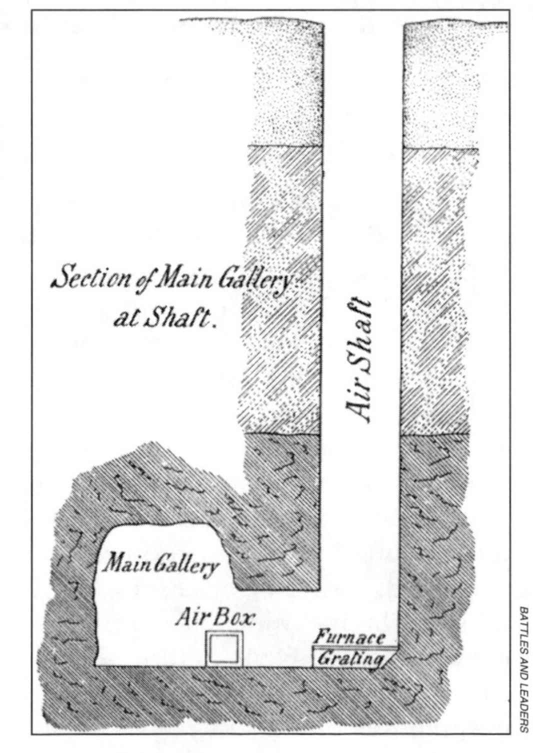

Cross section of the all-important main gallery at the air shaft. The furnace served to draw air into the tunnel.

BATTLES AND LEADERS

work, the diggers had to have fresh air, obtained only through vertical shafts that reached to the surface.

Pleasants and his engineers decided to experiment. They erected a large chimney at a spot where the Confederates could not see it, using discarded lumber to build what they boastfully called "the only long square wooden pipe in the western hemisphere, if not the entire world."

A clumsy section of heavy canvas functioned as a door of sorts, serving to make the main tunnel relatively airtight. Once this contrivance was in place, the wooden pipe was laid to connect the shaft beyond the "door" with the chimney outside. A brisk fire built in the chimney soon demonstrated that it could draw foul air from the end of the tunnel, while fresh air poured in through a separate section of wooden pipe.

Finally, the Pennsylvania miners, their commander, and their comrades accomplished their task. Two of the longest available fuses were spliced together and laid to reach 320 twenty-five-pound kegs of gunpowder that had been carefully tamped into place with sandbags. High-ranking officers approved detonation for the early hours of July 30, then they wrangled over what units would have the honor of leading the attack after the blast.

A division of African-American troops under the command of Brig. Gen. Edward Ferrero was designated to be the first to take advantage of the mammoth explosion. Grant or Meade or both, however, objected to this battle order. Should something go wrong, they pointed out, critics would charge that the black soldiers had been deliberately sacrificed due to the high risk involved.

The divisional commanders were ordered to conduct an informal lottery to decide who would have the honor of being first into what they called "the big hole." When James H. Ledlie won the draw, some of his colleagues were dismayed. He had already been pronounced by Grant to be inefficient, and soon he would be branded as a coward. To him fell the job of getting his men up what the Federals called Cemetery Hill and there forcing the Rebels to surrender. Brig. Gen. Joseph Haydn's division of the Army of the James was given its target, and Ferrero was told to follow Ledlie and his men. The black division was to rush past Cemetery Hill while it was under assault and reach the town of Petersburg, the focus of the lengthy siege operation.

With troops in readiness, waiting with beating hearts for the explosion, several minutes passed and nothing happened. Ruefully, the planners acknowledged that something must have gone wrong

When the dynamite in the tunnel was detonated, four tons of gunpowder exploded in one of the most awesome spectacles of the war. The blast created a hole 170 feet long, 60 to 80 feet wide, and 30 feet deep. Instead of forming around the crater and taking the Confederate line, Union troops rushed into the crater and were at the mercy of Southern artillery and riflemen. Grant called it a "stupendous failure."

with the spliced fuse. After a wait of about an hour, Lt. Jacob Douty and Sgt. Henry Rees of the Forty-eighth Pennsylvania volunteered to check the fuses. Crawling into the tunnel, they discovered that the fuse had failed after having burned about fifty feet.

Relighting it, the volunteers scrambled to the mouth of the tunnel as rapidly as they could and signaled their commander. Pleasants sent a courier to Burnside with word that the powder would explode in approximately eleven minutes.

The train of events that began at twelve minutes before 5:00 A.M. was described by more than one eyewitness. Capt. W. Gordon McCabe, a Confederate artillery officer, wrote: "A slight tremor of the earth for a second, then the rocking as of an earthquake, and with a tremendous burst which rent the sleeping hills beyond, a vast column of earth and smoke shoots upward to a great height, its dark sides flashing out sparks of fire, hangs poised for a moment in mid-air, and then hurtling downward with a roaring sound drops stones, broken timbers, and blackened human limbs before the gloomy pall of darkening smoke, flushing to an angry crimson, floats away to meet the morning sun." The "blackened human limbs" belonged to 278 Confederates who were killed in the blast.

Other units of men in gray stared in disbelief as the smoke began to clear, revealing an enormous hole just in front of their lines. On the spot, it received its name—the Crater—and became one of the best-known Civil War sites.

Days afterward measurements showed that eight thousand or more pounds of powder had created a hole that was 30 feet deep, at least 170 feet long, and its width varied from about 30 to more than 40 feet. Measured by any standard, the tunnel had done its work even better than the most optimistic miners anticipated.

For what seemed an eternity after the blast, nothing happened. Then all hell broke loose. Instead of forming around the crater, many of the Federals plunged into it and had no way of getting out in the face of suddenly vitalized Southerners shooting down on them. The black troops were ordered in, but it was too late.

By 1:00 P.M. the Federals had been pushed back to their lines. Union casualties were 3,798; Confederate losses about 1,500. Grant described the fiasco as a "stupendous failure." A court of inquiry was called. Burnside was relieved of command for improperly handling his troops. Ledlie, who had spent the whole time behind the action drinking rum in a bombproof, was criticized and then Meade read him out of the army. Ferrero, who had been with Ledlie, had his resignation accepted, but a bureaucratic mix-up gave him a major general's brevet for his conduct that day. He was then sent to an obscure post and after the war resumed his career as a dancing master. Pleasants and his hard-working miners were ignored.

16

Bennett H. Young

Yankee Gold on the Border

JOHN HAY, ONE OF Abraham Lincoln's private secretaries, wrote the only known description of Kentucky native George N. Sanders, one of the most elusive of Rebel secret agents. He seems to have worked undercover throughout the war, but his name does not appear in the *Official Records,* and Confederate documents—mostly postwar—include but half a dozen incidental references.

Hay, who went to Canada on an 1864 mission for his president, wrote only that "Sanders is a seedy-looking rebel with grizzled whiskers, and a flavor of old clo[thes]." Yet his influence, subterranean though it was, equaled that of many a general officer.

Lt. Bennett H. Young, also a Kentuckian, was a member of John Hunt Morgan's legendary cavalry and was captured with him during an 1863 Ohio raid. Escaping from the Ohio state penitentiary a few months afterward, Young disguised himself and made his way to Canada. Hailed there as a hero for the Southern cause, he soon became acquainted with Sanders and listened attentively as the secret agent unfolded what seemed to be a most attractive scheme.

Saint Albans, Vermont, lay within an easy three-hour ride of Canada and safety, Sanders pointed out. Although the town was small, it had more than one bank whose coffers should be bulging with gold stashed there by frugal New Englanders. A bank robbery by Confederate raiders would be front-page news throughout the Union, possibly disrupt Lincoln's reelection campaign, and ease some of the burden of the financially strapped Confederate government.

Young needed little persuasion to undertake the mission and recruit bank robbers from the Confederate refugees in Canada. Some of those he picked he had known earlier in Morgan's cavalry. Others appeared to be bold and willing to obey orders. Assured by Sanders that the mission had the approval of the Confederate government, Young proceeded to implement the raid. With a group of twenty raiders traveling by twos and threes, Young arrived at the Lafayette Hotel in Philipsburg, Canada, around October 11.

From the hotel employees the Confederates learned that nearby Saint Albans had three banks. To Young it seemed strange that a town with only three hundred or so homes should have so many financial establishments. All three of them, a desk clerk assured him, were not only solvent but prosperous. They were considered so safe that some Canadians used them.

Young prepared for his endeavor by stashing in his carpetbag small flasks filled with Greek fire, a phosphorus compound that would burst into flame when it was exposed to air. The plan called for the men to split up and take the train, the stagecoach, or ride to their target. Their second rendezvous would take place at the Tremont Hotel in Saint Albans, a lodging highly recommended by the citizens of Philipsburg. To avoid suspicion likely to be aroused by the arrival of so many strangers, the raiders were told to stay in boarding houses near the hotel and pose as vacationers and hunters.

Knowing that his men would begin arriving in town during the next three days, Young checked into the Tremont on October 15. After flashing a roll of currency, he was assigned to the largest room in the place, big enough for last-minute conferences.

Along with Lt. William Hutchinson, Young spent time inspecting the banks and deciding upon the best way to empty their coffers and return to Canada. To their surprise, they seemed to arouse no suspicion, nothing more than casual interest.

The raiders were given their final briefing when they filled Young's room on the evening of October 18. After being given their bottles of Greek fire, they coordinated their watches so that all could go into action precisely at 3:00 P.M. on the following day.

FRANK LESLIE'S ILLUSTRATED NEWSPAPER

Two tellers at the Saint Albans bank, hands raised, were required to take an oath of allegiance to the Confederacy.

At the appointed time Young reached the highest step in front of the American House Hotel, where he pulled out a revolver, waved it about, and shouted at the top of his lungs, "Saint Albans is now in the possession of the Confederate States of America!" A few passersby heard him clearly, but they laughed at the preposterous statement. He then crossed the street toward the First National Bank. Simultaneously, a trio of raiders converged upon the Saint Albans Bank, and a third group stepped to the door of the Franklin County Bank.

The raiders believed that the Franklin bank was the smallest of the three Saint Albans banks, but it had a walk-in vault. Before turning their attention to it, however, Young's men improvised and lost precious minutes by forcing the teller to swear allegiance to the Confederacy. The raiders then stuffed the money into their carpetbags, pushed the bank employees into the vault, and locked it.

At the Saint Albans Bank, plans went awry. The unexpected presence of a Federal soldier on leave caused the bank robbers to seize what was later described as "a mere pittance."

Young and his group did a great deal better at the First National Bank. Delighted to find the vault filled with bags of gold and silver and bundles of securities and currency, they were dismayed to realize that their three horses could not carry them and the heavy plunder.

With two pistols at his head, the teller obeyed the raiders' orders and asked no questions.

Some of the Confederates commandeered other animals, but precious time was lost.

This delay allowed a handful of residents to realize what was occurring. Several of them found their weapons and began shooting at the robbers, who returned fire, inflicting serious wounds on at least two civilians. No bank employee was injured in the melee.

Following the plan, as soon as all of his animals were loaded, Young led half of his men out of town. With the famous Rebel yell echoing down the main street, the robbers tossed the Greek fire right and left. The only structure they managed to destroy was a ramshackle woodshed.

Within minutes after the robbers began riding toward the Canadian border, the townspeople formed a posse and started in pursuit. When word of the raid flashed along telegraph lines, the governor of Vermont called out the home guard. In nearby New York State, Maj. Gen. John A. Dix offered a reward and announced that any raider who should come into his hands would immediately be hanged. The editor of the *Saint Albans Messenger* reported that depositors had lost "substantially more than $150,000 in hard money plus greenbacks."

Half a dozen of the Confederates were overtaken and captured a few minutes after they had crossed into Canada. Learning that they were likely to hang, Young decided to try to save his men's lives by surrendering himself. Members of the posse were in the process of hanging him when they were interrupted by a British major.

Announcing that the Vermonters were on "soil over which the queen alone has sovereignty," the major took charge of Young and led him to an impromptu stockade in Philipsburg where the other raiders were being held. Ignoring the protests of the U.S. authorities, British soldiers then took the captured raiders to Montreal. There at an extradition hearing, Judge Charles J. Coursol ruled that the bank robbery was "a hostile military expedition," which did not make its members felons. He released them on bond as internees.

In Washington, U.S. Secretary of War Edwin M. Stanton issued a statement about the findings of the Canadian court. Young and his men were bandits, he contended, and therefore were subject to immediate arrest when found on U.S. soil.

Canada's Parliament directed that fifty thousand dollars in gold be sent to Saint Albans to be divided among its banks. It was delivered after bank executives had discovered that the raiders had overlooked large quantities of gold coins and gold certificates. The raiders had been in such a hurry that they failed to find several bags that held more than one hundred thousand dollars in bonds and bank notes. More than fifty thousand dollars was overlooked at the Franklin County Bank. The captured raiders had made off with about eighty thousand dollars, all of which was eventually returned. As bank robberies go, the northernmost engagement of the Civil War was good for newspaper headlines—and little else.

Part 4

Nipped in the Bud

Abolitionist and orator Frederick Douglass refused to have anything to do with John Brown's grandiose scheme.

17

John Brown

Carving a New Nation

SOLDIERS WHO ANSWERED ABRAHAM Lincoln's call for volunteers marched into the Civil War singing the popular folk song on the martyrdom of abolitionist John Brown set to a rousing religious camp meeting tune: "John Brown's body lies a-mouldering in the grave, his soul goes marching on." In 1862, after she had visited military camps near Washington, D.C., Julia Ward Howe picked up the same melody for "The Battle Hymn of the Republic," which became the major war song of Union forces. Even as the twenty-first century dawns, scarcely a patriotic celebration is complete without a rousing rendition of her song by a massed choir.

In 1929 poet Stephen Vincent Benét won a Pulitzer Prize for his epic poem *John Brown's Body* in which he tried to give a complete picture of the controversial abolitionist. Who was this convicted felon who was hanged for treason and whose name lived on in song and story?

Revered throughout much of the North and universally despised in the South, Brown was born in West Torrington, Connecticut, the son of a cobbler and tanner. He spent many of his formative years in Ohio, where his father instilled in the growing boy an unforgiving hatred for slavery, an institution he was taught to regard as a great sin against God.

After brief schooling, at about age fifteen, Brown decided he wanted to be a minister, but lack of money put an end to that dream. Instead, he read the Bible for hours at a time and brooded over its majestic but sometimes mysterious passages.

Like his father, Brown became a tanner. After his marriage to Dianthe Lusk, he sired the first of her seven and his twenty children. While the fast-growing family lived in western Pennsylvania, Brown formed what he called an Independent Congregational Society from a little group of followers. He served as the preacher whenever members gathered on the second floor of his tannery, and he was noted for quoting long passages of the Bible to underscore his overt piety.

Then personal calamity struck. Dianthe fell into a prolonged depression that ended with her death. Stoic as always, Brown explained his loss as the will of God and soon took sixteen-year-old Mary Ann Day as his second wife. She bore thirteen offspring, but only six of them survived past their childhood years.

Brown experienced a midlife crisis that was possibly triggered by the panic of 1837, which bankrupted him. A series of attempts to get back on his feet financially failed, but he realized he could find meaning to life by fighting for a cause larger than himself. Living in Springfield, Massachusetts, he dedicated himself to the abolition of slavery and soon came to speak of himself as "an instrument of Providence."

In this role he persuaded a group of free black residents of Springfield to establish a defense league and make him its head. After brooding over the vivid story of Gideon in the Old Testament, he decided that the organization should be called the Branch of the United States League of Gileadites, and he began to formulate chaotic plans to free every slave in the nation.

Wealthy Gerrit Smith became an adherent and helped Brown to settle on one of his New York State holdings. Ralph Waldo Emerson and Henry David Thoreau knew Brown, and both of them expressed high esteem for him. Frederick Douglass, the most noted black leader of the period, was more cautious. Urged by Brown to become involved in his plot to do away with slavery, Douglass declined.

In 1855 he followed five of his sons to Kansas where they worked to keep the territory from becoming a slave state. He was barely settled there before he heard that slave owners from Missouri made frequent raids into Kansas, always making abolitionists their targets.

The ultimate offense in Brown's eyes was the May 1856 assault on the free-state community of Lawrence. Brown and his sons joined a band of free-staters intent on defending Lawrence, but the U.S. Army occupied the town and tried to keep the peace by keeping the free-staters out of Lawrence while the border ruffians withdrew.

At about the same time, news reached Kansas of violence in the U.S. Senate over slavery. Massachusetts Sen. Charles Sumner, the leading antislavery voice on Capitol Hill, was assaulted by a southern congressman, Preston Brooks of South Carolina. Brown was incensed by the news and determined to take action in any way he could.

It was said that some of the settlers along Pottawatomie Creek were active in the proslavery party. Rumor was good enough for Brown; without verifying the stories he heard, he conducted his first raid. Leading four of his sons and a small group of men, he saw to it that at least five settlers who lived along the creek went to their deaths on the night of May 24, 1856. Brown himself took an artillery sword and dismembered the bodies in front of the surviving family members.

The barbarity of the murders made Brown a marked man. Soon a band of armed men descended upon the Brown enclave, burning the cabins and killing one of Brown's sons, Frederick. This personal loss served to focus the abolitionist's purpose. His nebulous scheme aimed at freeing slaves turned into an elaborate plot to carve a new nation from the heart of the United States.

John Brown was clean-shaven until he became a wanted man following his raid on the Pottawatomie Creek settlement.

Such an ambitious plot could not succeed without sufficient money. Operating in strict secrecy, Brown persuaded Gerrit Smith and another man of means, George L. Stearns, to back him financially. Soon two distinguished ministers added their support: Theodore Parker and Thomas Wentworth Higginson. Years later Higginson commanded the First South Carolina Colored Infantry, the first African-American regiment raised to fight for the Union. Dr. Samuel Gridley Howe, husband of Julia Ward Howe, was the fifth member of the secret committee that provided funds to transform Brown's plot from fantasy into action.

During the spring of 1858 many adherents and some who were merely curious accepted Brown's invitation to meet in Chatham, Canada. There, for the first time, he publicly announced his plan. From a base in the Appalachian Mountains, he would form a new nation from which slavery would be barred forever. His listeners gave hearty assent to what he termed a constitution for the new nation, and they chose him to serve as its commander in chief.

A year later Brown and a score of his most dedicated followers went into action. Weapons stored at Harpers Ferry, Virginia (now West Virginia), were considered crucial to Brown's success. Hence he rented a nearby farm and began final preparations for an assault upon the important U.S. armory, arsenal, and rifle works.

Members of the secret band struck on the night of October 16, 1860, and quickly gained possession of the armory, other buildings, and the bridges that led to the village. As insurance against a counterassault, Brown took several prominent citizens as hostages, including Col. Louis Washington, a great-grandnephew of George Washington. Within hours, he reasoned, word of his accomplishments would reach plantations in Virginia and Maryland. Soon hordes of slaves would flock to his banner. After providing these recruits with weapons seized from the armory, Brown's Army of God would fan out and conquer the vast tract of land on which their new nation would be created.

To Brown's surprise, the expected slave uprising did not materialize. Instead, the townspeople—soon to be supported by units of the Virginia militia—began exchanging shots with the men who thought themselves secure in the government buildings. Brown and his men were driven into the engine house, and three local men were killed. Word of the takeover brought quick action in the nation's capital. President Franklin Buchanan ordered U.S. Marines into action under the command of Lt. Col. Robert E. Lee.

FRANK LESLIE'S ILLUSTRATED NEWSPAPER

U.S. Marines commanded by Lt. Col. Robert E. Lee of the U.S. Army storm the engine house where Brown and his raiders held several hostages.

The federal contingent arrived at first light the next morning. Moving swiftly, Lee first demanded Brown's surrender and then stormed the refuge when that was turned down. When the fight was over, a wounded Brown was captured along with five of his raiders. The rest, including two of Brown's sons, were dead or had fled.

Less than forty-eight hours after his seizure of the buildings, Brown was headed toward Charles Town, Virginia, in shackles. Soon a formal indictment was drawn up, charging the abolitionist with "treason to the Commonwealth of Virginia" and entering into a conspiracy to lead an uprising of slaves.

During his trial, whose outcome was never in doubt, his relatives and friends produced affidavits declaring the leader of the plot to be insane. Gov. Henry A. Wise received seventeen such documents but refused to commute the death sentence that had been imposed.

Brown showed remarkable equanimity throughout the proceedings, defending himself by attacking slavery. He took the verdict of the court calmly. "Let them hang me," he said. "I am worth inconceivably

FRANK LESLIE'S ILLUSTRATED NEWSPAPER

At Charles Town, Virginia, Brown refused the customary hood and climbed the gallows with wide-open eyes.

more to hang than for any other purpose." That appraisal proved to be prophetic. He was hanged December 2, 1859.

Abolitionists now had a martyr as well as a cause. In much of the North, men formerly reluctant to think of civil war began openly to espouse a call to arms. As much as any other individual except Abraham Lincoln, Brown influenced the course taken by Americans already divided into hostile regional groups.

18

Charles Wilkes

Minus Four Passengers

RECALLED FROM THE COAST of Africa for an undisclosed mission—perhaps the Federal assault upon Port Royal, South Carolina—the sloop of war USS *San Jacinto* lurched across the Atlantic Ocean in October 1861. Charles Wilkes, her captain, was hopeful. Perhaps, at last, he would be given a chance to give the Rebels such a hard blow that he would gain the adulation he deserved!

During forty-four years in the U.S. Navy, Wilkes had acquired a reputation as being ambitious and unscrupulous. Many of his officers and most of his crew hated him. Aware of their attitude and caring not a whit what they thought, the harsh disciplinarian drove his men mercilessly.

During a period of extremely high seas on the westward voyage of his 1,567-ton warship, Wilkes spent a great deal of time in his cabin. He brooded over having been forced against his wishes to take part the past April in the burning of the Gosport Navy Yard. He would have preferred to fight to the last man rather than put the torch to the finest facility of its sort held by the U.S. Navy.

Now surely he would be given command of a new ironclad, leaving his obsolete wooden vessel. A promotion would be likely, he concluded, and he might send Johnny Reb whimpering back to the land of cotton.

Charles Wilkes as a commander in the U.S. Navy.

BASED ON A BRADY STUDIO PORTRAIT

In late October, Wilkes stopped at Cienfuegos, Cuba, to take on coal, water, and provisions. There he heard a rumor that caused him to become as narrowly directed as a fine hunting dog at the first scent of quarry. Two former U.S. senators, now Confederate diplomatic envoys, were somewhere in Cuban waters. John Slidell, a New Yorker who had moved to New Orleans after his business failed during the War of 1812, was on his way to represent the South in France. James M. Mason of Virginia bore credentials to be presented to the British.

If Wilkes could capture that pair, his career would be transformed instantly. It was well known in Havana that Mason, Slidell, and some companions expected to sail for Saint Thomas on November 7 aboard the English mail steamer *Trent,* headed for a British port. "I made up my mind," Wilkes later reported to the secretary of the navy, Gideon Welles, "to await a suitable position on the route of the steamer to intercept her and take them [the Confederates] out."

A quick run to Key West in search of help proved futile; the *Powhatan* and other U.S. warships had already departed that port. This left Wilkes "disappointed and obliged to rely upon the vigilance of the officer and crew" of his vessel only. Stopping briefly on the northern coast of Cuba, the Federal officer received another disappointment. In reply to a telegram, the British consul Joseph T. Crawford reported from

The *San Jacinto,* as depicted by German artist Isodor Rocca.

Havana that he had no firm knowledge about the date on which the *Trent* would sail. Wilkes would have to lurk and wait while relishing the idea of seizing the Confederate diplomats and taking the *Trent* as a prize of war whose value would be divided among him and his crew.

By the time an approaching steamer was spotted at 11:40 A.M. on November 8, Wilkes was already contemplating the Thanks of Congress for his bold and imaginative stroke against the Rebels. "We were all prepared for [the *Trent*]," he confided to Welles, "[hence] beat to quarters, and orders were given to Lieut. D. M. Fairfax to have two boats manned and armed to board her and make Messrs. Slidell, Mason [and their secretaries] prisoners and send them immediately on board [the *San Jacinto*]." Wilkes said nothing about having hauled down the U.S. flag so it would not be seen from the deck of his quarry. When the *Trent* approached, flying British colors, the Federal vessel hoisted its own emblem and simultaneously fired a shot across the bow of the English vessel.

"She maintained her speed and showed no disposition to heave to," Wilkes reported. A second shot proved convincing, and a cutter

LIBRARY OF CONGRESS

Although he was given top billing at the time, James Slidell later became known as the second member of the Mason and Slidell expedition.

was dispatched under Lieutenant Fairfax. Confronting Capt. James Moir as soon as he stepped aboard, Fairfax demanded the passenger list. Moir only shook his head and made what Fairfax interpreted as a threatening gesture.

Alarmed, Fairfax dispatched part of his boarding party back to their warship to ask for assistance. In response, Lt. James A. Greer and an armed party arrived beside the *Trent.* In the meantime, Slidell and Mason had been recognized "and told they were required to go aboard" the *San Jacinto.*

When they resisted, two or three sailors "used a little force" to put them and their secretaries aboard the warship about 2:00 P.M. It took another ninety minutes to bring the papers and baggage of the captives aboard, after which "the *Trent* was suffered to proceed on her route to the eastward."

The release of the vessel instead of taking her to a prize court was a last-minute change of plans. Wilkes later explained that he had two considerations. To take the English vessel into port as a prize of war, he would have to man her with members of his own crew, which would have "weakened the strength of the San Jacinto's battery in the upcoming struggle at Port Royal, South Carolina." Also, he found there were a number of women and children aboard the *Trent,* and their schedules would have been disrupted had he seized the ship.

LIBRARY OF CONGRESS

James M. Mason's seizure created a firestorm of anger against the United States in England.

Wilkes steamed to Saint Augustine and then to Charleston. From officers of the Federal fleet then blockading the South Carolina port, he was disappointed to learn that he had missed the assault on Port Royal and Hilton Head.

One week after having scored what he considered to be perhaps the greatest coup of the war, Wilkes reached Hampton Roads. There he received orders to convey Slidell and Mason to Fort Warren at Boston. When he reached that port he glowed as he read a telegram from the secretary of the navy, which said in part:

> I congratulate you on your safe arrival, and especially do I congratulate you on the great public service you have rendered in the capture of the rebel emissaries. Messrs. Mason and Slidell have been conspicuous in the conspiracy to dissolve the Union and it is well known that when seized by you they were on a mission hostile to the Government and the country. Your conduct in seizing these public enemies was marked by intelligence, ability, decision and firmness and has the emphatic approval of this Department.

Wilkes happily consigned his former prisoners to the care of Col. Justin Dimick, commandant at Fort Warren.

Soon Northern newspapers were filled with praise of the man who had prevented the Confederate diplomats from reaching their posts. Instead of the Thanks of Congress that Wilkes expected, the lawmakers rose and cheered as they voted to bestow a special gold medal on him. Only an occasional word of caution was expressed about what naval experts branded "a highly unusual procedure upon the open seas." From Detroit the former governor of the Michigan Territory sent a telegram to Secretary of State William H. Seward. Having been minister to France and secretary of both war and state, Lewis Cass expressed anxiety over a war with England.

When the Cass telegram of December 19 reached the capital, Seward was beginning to wonder at the British silence. He had received no communication whatever about the matter from Lord Lyon, the British ambassador to the United States. Nevertheless, Seward was among those who offered personal congratulations to Wilkes.

Abraham Lincoln expressed pleasure that "so-called secessionist envoys had been stopped in their tracks." Although the Trent affair was discussed at several cabinet meetings, the president was inclined to scoff at notions of British retaliation.

Ohio Gov. Thomas Ewing sent word to the chief executive that he did not think it a wise policy "to insist on extending the rights of belligerents over neutral vessels on the high seas." John Hay, one of the president's secretaries, transmitted the Ewing telegram to Seward with a sarcastic notation regarding "Mr. Ewing's dissertation on neutral rights."

In England and on the Continent—fourteen days away by ship—news of the exploit created a tremendous uproar. Edouard A. Thouvenel of France castigated Wilkes and his action in the public press. Count Albrecht Bernstorff took the same stance in Berlin. Earl John Russell, head of the British foreign office, made no secret of his fury.

Details of the *Trent* affair soon circulated throughout England. Richard Williams, the vessel's mail officer, angrily reported that the Americans had ignored his protests despite the fact that he wore the uniform of a commander in the Royal Navy. An editorial in the London *Times* condemned Wilkes, saying, "Swagger and ferocity, built on a foundation of vulgarity and cowardice, are his characteristics, and these are the most prominent marks by which his countrymen, generally speaking, are known around the world."

Public resentment was so great that Russell and his colleagues took action more swiftly than usual. Troops numbering between eight thousand and twelve thousand were ordered to Canada at once. A shipment of saltpeter, desperately needed by the Du Pont powder factory for the

Charles F. Adams Sr., as satirized in *Vanity Fair.*

Union war effort, was halted. Telegrams were sent to all crown officials in North America, warning of a war with the United States.

Charles Francis Adams Sr., the U.S. minister in London, dispatched a series of frantic reports to Washington. He had never seen the city so aroused, he said, and he later admitted that he expected to be ordered to leave the kingdom.

Although Queen Victoria was inclined to follow the advice of Lord Russell and send a stern ultimatum to Washington, her consort, Prince Albert, persuaded her to soften her language. He was, however, unable to stop the preparations taking place in Canada. Adams advised the State Department that there was nothing he could do to prevent the expected conflict.

Following instructions from Russell, Ambassador Lyons advised Secretary Seward that Britain would consent to a delay of one week. If the issue were not settled, the British legation was to leave Washington "to repair immediately to London."

PUNCH

British attitudes were depicted in a cartoon showing Britannia, lanyard in hand, waiting to reply to diplomatic demands concerning the *Trent* affair.

On December 26, Seward dispatched an extremely long message to Lyons summarizing and defending Wilkes's actions. Concerning the four Southerners taken from the *Trent* by force, he concluded with three short sentences that amounted to complete capitulation by the United States: "The four persons in question are now held in military custody at Fort Warren, in the state of Massachusetts. They will be cheerfully liberated. Your lordship will please indicate a time and a place for receiving them." Because Seward bowed to the inevitable and convinced Lincoln to do the same, the international turmoil stirred up by Wilkes soon subsided.

At noon on January 1, 1862, the Confederates were escorted from Fort Warren and returned to the protection of the British flag. Mason, Slidell, and two secretaries were ushered aboard HMS *Rinaldo,* where they were treated like celebrities during their two-week voyage to England. There Mason coordinated some purchases for Confederate agents, raised some money in the private sector for his cause, but was never received officially by the British government. In France, Slidell was unable to get military aid or a treaty of alliance. Ambassador Adams did not return home but rather exerted significant influence among Britain's leaders.

Humiliated and angry, Wilkes retired to the *San Jacinto* and refused to see members of the press. There is no record that the gold medal voted him by Congress was ever minted or presented. Through newspaper reports, Wilkes learned the dismal truth about what he had considered the perfect scheme. It was not his successful effort to halt the voyage of the Confederates but his seizure of passengers from a British vessel that had created the furor.

Experts in international law focused upon a fundamental issue in discussing the case. Had Wilkes seized the *Trent* and taken her to a prize court for adjudication of issues, England would have had no basis for a protest. Wilkes later learned the British vessel carried $1.5 million in gold and silver. All of it, as well as the value of the vessel and her other cargo, might have been awarded to him and his crew had she been taken to a Federal port instead of allowed to go on her way minus just four passengers.

19

Sons of Liberty

The Great Northwest Conspiracy

ONE OF THE BOLDEST plots of the late war was launched precisely twenty-five years ago. Members of a new generation need to be reminded of it, and this anniversary is a good time to do so." That statement in 1889 in the *Philadelphia Press* introduced readers to this account:

> Colonel T. A. Burr, a well-known Confederate officer, tells the story of an attempt to release 20,000 prisoners at Chicago, Columbus, and Sandusky in 1864, and to form a northwestern confederacy. Major C. H. Cole of the Fifth Tennessee regiment, was the leading spirit of the plot. He narrowly escaped hanging, and is now a prominent railroad man in Texas. He received his instructions from Jacob Thompson, who was then in Canada, and was put in command of the department of Ohio, with headquarters at Sandusky. With the force of the 20,000 Rebels whom the conspirators intended to release, and with the active aid of Northern sympathizers, it was thought that a northwestern conspiracy was not impossible; and the time fixed for the assault on the camps where the prisoners were confined was gauged by [Confederate] General Early's attack on Washington, which was to engage the great force of our army, and make it impossible to reinforce the small

> body of Union soldiers in the Northwest, where there was almost open rebellion against conscription, and people were weary of war. It was first intended to strike the blow while the National Democratic Convention was in session in Chicago, and more than 4,000 Confederate soldiers and sympathizers were there ready for action. But, Early's delay in striking Washington caused a postponement [that led to abandonment of the elaborate scheme].

Slightly different versions of this story appeared in countless northern newspapers, whose readers lacked the resources to test its accuracy. Some details were correct, but there were numerous flaws in the postwar account.

The *Official Records* do not mention a Col. T. A. Burr, perhaps a fictional name chosen because Aaron Burr was an infamous traitor. Former Confederate Gen. Jubal Early issued a refutation of this version of "the Northwest Conspiracy" and its purported timing to coincide with his assault upon Washington. Camp Douglas, at Chicago, probably held less than ten thousand Southerners when the prison's population was at its peak.

It is true that the last desperate attempt to foment insurrection in the Northwest, a region known today as the Midwest, was expected to take place when the Democrats converged in Chicago for their 1864 convention. It is also true that Columbus and Sandusky in Ohio were

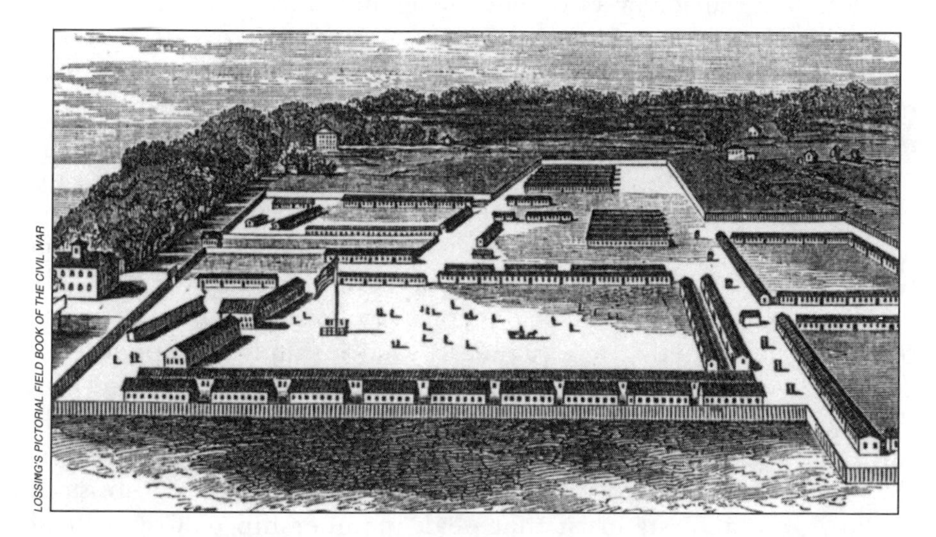

Chicago's Camp Douglas sprawled over many acres.

LIBRARY OF CONGRESS

Any Northerner who espoused peace was regarded as a Copperhead and was likely to be depicted as a serpent.

involved in the elaborate plot, which seems really to have been masterminded from Canada by a Confederate agent named Jacob Thompson.

The summary concerning "Major C. H. Cole" reveals, however, how distorted the Northern account was. Cole was a captain, not a major. Far from being "the leading spirit of the plot," Cole was a member of the Confederate party that made an unsuccessful attempt to capture the USS *Michigan*. Captured in September 1864, and charged with piracy, Cole was expected to go on trial as "a public spy."

Northerners who openly sympathized with or supported the Confederacy did so in a variety of ways. Some of them were Knights of the Golden Circle, while others belonged to the Sons of Liberty. Members of both secret societies were popularly known simply as Copperheads. There are no reliable records on which to base reports concerning the size of these pro-Confederate organizations. In Richmond, Jefferson Davis and his aides believed the number of these Southern sympathizers in the North to be in the range of six hundred thousand. Today, some analysts insist that peak membership of Copperhead groups ranged around thirty-five thousand.

Davis appointed Thompson and Clement Clay as agents in Canada, where they were expected to spend "a substantial sum" to foster subversive activities in the northwestern United States. In Richmond it became an article of faith that forces directed by these men would easily succeed in sabotaging railroads and steamers. False stories planted in Northern newspapers were expected to magnify the results actually achieved.

From this scheme there evolved an elaborate plot to liberate prisoners of war and "call true patriots to arms" to take control of Illinois and parts of Ohio and Indiana. Although presumably approved in Richmond, the Thompson enterprise was about as carefully contrived and as likely of success as was John Brown's plot to form a new nation.

Capt. Thomas Hines—not Cole—was selected to head the Confederates who would make Chicago their first great target. The fifty-seven men led by Hincs split up into parties of two, three, or four and took separate routes toward their rendezvous point.

One man, a Union agent named Thomas Keefe, effectively defeated the first move upon Chicago and Camp Douglas. Riding a train from Canada in company with a few of the raiders, Keefe learned many details of the plot. Once in Chicago, Keefe hurried to the office of Col. Benjamin Sweet, commander of the prison camp that then held about eight thousand Confederates. When the colonel learned

NATIONAL ARCHIVES

Benjamin Sweet was the commandant at Camp Douglas.

that the men in his custody might receive outside aid in an attempted prison break, he immediately brought in two thousand Union soldiers to serve as guards. An alert from Sweet to the police commissioners of Chicago resulted in the arrest of Judge Buckner S. Morris and other prominent men who were known to be Copperheads.

When Hines reached Chicago, he called for his own kind of troops. Chapters of the Sons of Liberty were within fifty miles of Chicago, and he expected no less than five thousand volunteers. While the Union soldiers, who were under orders, moved quickly to surround Camp Douglas, the Copperheads, who had no command structure, casually ignored Hines's summons to action.

This state of affairs failed to lead to "the explosion designed to shake the Union and to form a strong new ally of the Confederacy." Instead, the plot simply fizzled out. Cole, whose involvement was distant and peripheral, was one of the few conspirators to be identified and arrested. Hines and most of those who followed him from Canada simply faded into obscurity and vanished.

This denouement should have quashed for all time the myth that the Confederate plot to take over the Northwest almost succeeded. That the tale was still very much alive twenty-five years later is due not to military but to political factors.

With the election of 1864 approaching, no man in America knew better than Abraham Lincoln that its outcome was in doubt. Although largely self-taught, he was one of the most skillful political leaders ever to emerge in the United States.

Lincoln levied "patriotic contributions" from most people on the Federal payroll. These assessments went into the war chest of the Republican Party—whose name was briefly changed to the National Union Party. Also, dozens of prominent Democrats had been given commissions as general officers in the Federal forces, so the Democratic leadership structure was significantly weakened. As an additional measure to ensure reelection, the president took an unprecedented administrative step. Preparing a paper that bound persons signing it to serve faithfully under whoever might win the Executive Mansion in November 1864, Lincoln presented it to his cabinet members without revealing its contents. They dutifully signed this strange document and did not learn what they had pledged themselves to do until later.

Because many Republicans felt that it was time to replace Lincoln with an outspoken advocate of peace, his adherents were seeking something to discredit his Democratic opposition. Circulation of the greatly embellished story of the failed Northwestern Conspiracy was just the propaganda tool they sought.

Indiana Gov. Oliver P. Morton made deliberate use of "the Rebel threat to seize control of the entire northwest." There were a substantial number of Hoosier Copperheads, and Morton correctly reasoned that their movement would be squelched when loyal citizens were told that the Northwest Conspiracy was gigantic in its scope. Other elected officials used the exaggerated tale to strengthen their own positions, but none were so adroit in exploiting it as was Morton.

Today the story of the Northwest Conspiracy is still treated seriously in some history textbooks. Yet the consensus of informed opinion is that it had little or no impact upon the outcome of the struggle.

20

Jubal Anderson Early

The Late Raid

MAJ. GEN. JUBAL ANDERSON Early radiated the enthusiasm that caused many of his men to speak of him affectionately as "Old Jube" and "Old Jubal." As he assessed the situation, the time was ripe for the big move he had been advocating for some time. After exchanging warm greetings, he sat down with Jefferson Davis and Robert E. Lee.

Davis would have welcomed an opportunity to serve as a field commander instead of president of the Confederate States of America. Like Abraham Lincoln, he made occasional forays into the field. It was known that Davis considered the afternoon of July 21, 1861, to have been one of his finest hours. Barely established in Richmond, he had learned that the anticipated big battle was under way in the vicinity of Manassas Junction, so he hurried there to savor the Southern victory. His chief disappointment, he confessed after the Federal forces retreated toward safety, was the failure of the Confederate forces to march upon Washington.

During weary month after weary month that followed Bull Run, as the Federals called the Manassas battle, Davis never gave up the notion that a fast-moving force could someday seize the U.S. capital and thereby bring an end to the war. Meanwhile, in Washington City,

Approaching the outskirts of the Federal capital, Jubal Early was momentarily intoxicated with joy.

Lincoln agonized over the probability that the Confederates would someday strike there.

Lincoln's concern for the safety of his capital was so great that it became a major source of friction between the commander in chief and his top military officers. Time and time again, the president demanded that troops be deployed for its defense despite protests by his generals that they were needed in action elsewhere.

Until he backed the promotion of Ulysses S. Grant to the rank of lieutenant general, the president had functioned literally as the commander in chief of Union forces. He demanded and received the best military engineers available and instructed them about the placement and design of the fortifications he wanted for the protection of Washington. Lincoln's activities were well known in Richmond, but this did not discourage Early, who had long had the enemy capital in mind as a target.

Born and reared in Virginia, Old Jube fought in the Seminole Wars after his 1837 graduation from West Point. He then resigned his commission to study and practice law, but he returned to the military

Fiery abolitionist Union Gen. David Hunter was ridiculed and despised by Rebel leaders.

PHOTOGRAPHIC HISTORY OF THE CIVIL WAR

during the Mexican War. When the Virginia convention met in April 1861 to consider severing the Old Dominion from the United States of America, Early voted against secession. Once his state took steps to leave the Union, however, he went into uniform for the third time and fought at First Manassas as colonel of the Twenty-fourth Virginia Infantry. For many months he was present during nearly all the significant engagements of the Army of Northern Virginia.

After the second battle of Cold Harbor in June 1864, Robert E. Lee sent Early, now a lieutenant general, into the Shenandoah Valley to face Union Maj. Gen. David Hunter. Labeled by the Confederate Congress "a felon to be executed if captured," Hunter was responsible for what Southerners considered wanton destruction. He had burned the buildings of the Virginia Military Institute and the residence of Gov. John Letcher before launching what would today be termed a scorched-earth policy.

At their meeting on June 12, 1864, Davis, Lee, and Early agreed upon a tentative course of action. Following that plan, Early and his men raced toward Charlottesville on the following morning. Hunter, who had been advancing against Lynchburg, was pursued beyond the town of Salem before moving toward the mountains of West Virginia and safety.

LIBRARY OF CONGRESS

Federal Gen. Lew Wallace held up Early's advance at the Monocacy River in Maryland until Union troops recalled from Petersburg could man the forts around the Northern capital.

At this point, a telegram from Lee left it to Early's discretion whether or not to proceed with the second phase of their plan and move upon Washington. According to his subordinates, Early's reaction was of "unadulterated glee," and fourteen thousand men in gray soon were headed toward the Federal capital.

Union Maj. Gen. Lewis Wallace of the Army of the Potomac threw an unexpected obstacle into the path of the Confederates when his Eighth Corps planted themselves squarely across the path Early intended to take at Monocacy, Maryland. The battle there on July 9, 1864, lasted most of the day, and Early correctly reported victory. He lost fewer than seven hundred men while inflicting almost two thousand Union casualties and driving Wallace from the field. Reporting that he did not wish to have his movements hampered by prisoners, Early did not pursue his foes toward Baltimore.

The men in gray did not know it, but the one-day delay at Monocacy radically altered the prospects of the Davis-Lee-Early scheme. A few all-important hours gave Federal authorities time to act. Lincoln let Grant know that he was urgently needed in the capital, but Grant felt the siege of Petersburg was too important to be interrupted.

Hunter, ordered by Grant to move to defend Washington, reported that his most rapid avenue—the Ohio River—was incapable of floating

Visibly careworn, at Fort Stevens the president showed wanton disregard for his own safety.

NATIONAL ARCHIVE

his army to the capital in time. Grant next turned to Brig. Gen. Horatio Gouverneur Wright. The Nineteenth Corps was en route from Louisiana to join the Army of the Potomac, and Grant ordered these veterans to go straight to the capital. Riding at the head of his troops, Wright reached Washington about noon on July 11. By nightfall his forces were established within the capital's fortifications.

Lt. Asa T. Abbott of the U.S. Signal Corps was one of many men in blue who witnessed one of the most extraordinary events that took place during the war. Rebel forces had moved along Washington's Seventh Street Pike until their advance was stopped six miles from the capital by massive Fort Stevens. Halting at a distance of only 250 yards, the Confederates took occasional shots at men on the parapet.

Shortly after noon a fast-moving carriage was driven to the sally port. Although Abbott may not have known it, Lincoln had visited the installation the previous day, and some accounts record that he came under fire then. If that was the case, it made little difference in the conduct of the man from Illinois.

Artist Francis B. Carpenter and Mary Lincoln are known to have been in the carriage with Lincoln on Monday. No one noticed if either accompanied the president when he strode up to the parapet. Standing within a few feet of Abbott, Lincoln asked for a field glass and seemed to be making a careful inspection of the enemy forces. He was not sufficiently familiar with them to identify four infantry divisions, each of which had a major general at its head: Robert E. Rodes, John C. Breckinridge, Stephen Dodson Ramseur, and John B. Gordon. Abbott's summary of events noted:

> The officers then told [the president] that he had better get down from the parapet, but he did not move or reply. A moment later an officer went to him & told him that he *must* get down as the enemy was with easy range. Again there was no response. However, an assistant surgeon rushed to Mr. Lincoln and took a stand at his left. He had not been there more than half a minute before he took a ball in his leg. Mr. Lincoln saw what had happened, so got down from his vantage point as deliberately as he had climbed to it. Returning to his carriage, he mounted its step, entered, and was soon out of sight.

Some details not preserved by Abbott appear in other accounts of the only time a sitting president has ever come under enemy fire. One of these is that a young officer raced toward the president and yelled at the top of his voice, "Get down, you fool!" The officer was Oliver Wendell Holmes Jr., son of the poet and later a U.S. Supreme Court justice.

Having satisfied himself that Fort Stevens was formidable but lightly manned, Early sent out scouts to seek a weak point in the ring of defenses that protected Washington. A council of war was held with his four division commanders, one of whom had learned that the Sixth Corps was now firmly established in the capital. Another warned that an unknown but large number of men under Emory would nearly double the size of defending forces during the night. There was nothing he could do against such odds, Early realized. Hence he ruefully informed his aides that they would be forced to withdraw but would remain visible during the early hours of July 12 "in order to let the enemy know what might have happened."

Lincoln paid a return visit to Fort Stevens while the Confederates were still in sight and watched with satisfaction as they raced for cover when blue-clad columns began moving out from the line of fortresses. Pushing through Rockville and Poolesville, men in gray crossed the Potomac River near Leesburg and headed back toward the Shenandoah Valley.

Years later Early claimed that his relatively small force faced more than fifty-three thousand men in blue. Summarizing the scheme that never matured, the Confederate wrote: "If the Federal commanders in Washington and General Hunter had been possessed of the requisite enterprise and daring it would have been impossible for me to have escaped the capture of my entire command. All my movements were based on the presumed want of enterprise on the part of the enemy, and it seems that Federal commanders cannot understand the audacity that caused their Capital to be threatened by so small a force."

Part 5

Much Ado about Nearly Nothing

LESLIE'S ILLUSTRATED HISTORY OF THE CIVIL WAR

The burning of the merchantman *Harvey Birch* in the British Channel on November 17, 1861, could be seen from the British mainland and raised the issue of whether or not the North could protect its ships on the high seas.

21

Robert B. Pegram

Destination London

SINCE SOME OF THE documents relating to the transatlantic voyage of the CSS *Nashville* are missing, only a few details about plans set in motion in Richmond are known for certain. James Mason and John Slidell were officially accredited to represent the Confederacy in England and France, respectively. With the Federal blockade beginning to create serious problems, Southern leaders felt it unwise to send diplomatic representatives abroad on a blockade-runner. Therefore the two diplomats sailed aboard the British mail steamer *Trent*.

Since the mission of the two agents was known in Washington, there was danger that the *Trent* might be stopped at sea. Hence Lt. Robert B. Pegram was ordered to maneuver his vessel, the CSS *Nashville,* to draw Federal warships away from the *Trent*. When the plans were being formulated, this may have been the primary mission of the Rebel vessel.

While headed east by northeast, Pegram managed to lure at least three Union ships into pursuing him. Once he eluded the last of them, he may have developed what he regarded as an important scheme. Instead of returning to Confederate waters, he sailed for England. Should he reach the British capital, he calculated that his bold demonstration of Confederate naval power would bring diplomatic recognition to his homeland.

He did not anticipate any use of his guns, but he kept them ready. Although they were not needed, he soon had a little excitement which he detailed in his ship's log:

> At 9:00 on the morning of the 19th November [1861] a sail was sighted standing toward us, which proved to be the [Yankee] clipper ship *Harvey Birch,* Captain M. Nelson, from [Le] Havre to New York, in ballast [without a commercial cargo]. When within hailing distance, I hoisted the Confederate flag and demanded the surrender of the vessel as a prize to the *Nashville,* which demand was instantly complied with. I then ordered the captain to come on board with his ship's papers, and after a careful examination of these, one of the officers of the *Nashville* went on board of the *Harvey Birch,* and after transferring the officers and crew (thirty-one in number) on board the *Nashville,* with their personal effects, set the *Harvey Birch* on fire. Before she was lost to our sight her masts had gone by the board and she had burned to the water's edge. I then continued my course, and on 21st November anchored off the port of Southampton, the officers and crew of the *Harvey Birch* being liberated and permitted to go on shore.

Pegram's summary fails to capture the high-adventure aspects of this international incident in which he was central. His vessel seized and burned the merchantman within the English Channel, so close to land that smoke from the *Harvey Birch* was seen in three or four British cities.

His destruction of an empty Northern-owned vessel estimated to be worth $150,000 is all but forgotten now; however, when it took place it created a sensation. From New York, T. B. Satterthwaite, the president of a board of insurance underwriters, telegraphed the Executive Mansion, urging the president to order "armed steamers of sufficient power" to cruise in "the British and Irish channels and off the Straits of Gibraltar."

Urgent as the matter was, Abraham Lincoln's hands seemed to have been tied. Most available Union vessels had been assigned to the blockade of Southern ports. Also, the president and his aides were engrossed with a much more threatening issue, the *Trent* affair. The British vessel had been stopped by a U.S. warship on the high seas and four passengers—Mason, Slidell, and their secretaries—taken prisoners. As a result, the English threatened war.

From Southampton, Pegram reported with great delight that "there appears to be a great probability of an early rupture between

England and the United States." That failed to materialize, however, after the U.S. government released the Confederate passengers. Nevertheless, many people in England made little effort to hide their sympathy for the Confederacy. The prime minister, Lord Palmerston, paid a visit to the *Nashville* after she was moored in the Thames.

Stormy weather encountered on her voyage across the Atlantic had left the *Nashville* crippled. Her wheelhouses, guards, bulwarks, and part of her hurricane deck had been washed away by heavy seas. As a result, she went into dry dock on December 5. Attempting to show that his fledgling nation was a genuine ally of Great Britain, Pegram ordered his Confederate flag to fly at half-mast when Queen Victoria's husband, Prince Albert, died on December 14, although the prince had been strongly opposed to Britain's aiding the Confederacy.

Reports from London to the U.S. secretary of the navy, Gideon Welles, indicated that the British authorities were showing the Confederates every courtesy. Far more serious in the eyes of Washington, however, was the fact that U.S. Ambassador Charles Francis Adams was rebuffed when he tried to persuade the British to hold Pegram and his men as pirates. Instead, they were given safe haven.

Increasingly uneasy about foreign reactions to the voyage of the *Nashville,* Welles took matters into his own hands. While the Confederate vessel was dry-docked for repairs, Pegram received alarming news that a Union warship was en route. Comdr. Tunis R. M. Craven of the USS *Tuscarora* had orders to seek and destroy the *Nashville.* Although warned to "avoid trespassing on neutral rights," Craven was enjoined to be firm in exercising U.S. rights. Specific details were left to Craven's discretion, for the secretary of the navy said, "What course may be taken by the English authorities with the *Nashville,* a vessel without a recognized flag or authority, which had been guilty of the piratical act of capturing and burning the merchant ship of a nation at peace with that government and the world, and then seeking refuge in her ports, we have at present no means of ascertaining."

According to the Confederates, the arrival of the *Tuscarora* off Southampton caused great indignation. To prevent the Union warship from attacking the Confederate vessel in British waters, the authorities ordered both Craven and Pegram to depart. The *Nashville* was to leave immediately, but the harbor authorities delayed permitting the *Tuscarora* to sail until twenty-four hours had passed. In the event Craven tried to ignore this order, the English frigate *Shannon* pulled alongside the U.S. vessel "with steam up and guns shotted."

The *Nashville* left Southampton on February 3. High winds caused the vessel to use much of its coal, and Pegram abandoned the original plan of sailing to Charleston or Savannah in favor of Saint George, Bermuda. Leaving that port on February 24, Pegram set out for Beaufort, North Carolina. In addition to filling its coal bunkers at Saint George, the Confederate vessel picked up a pilot who was familiar with Beaufort waters.

En route the *Nashville* captured the schooner *Robert Gilfillan,* out of Philadelphia and bound for Haiti with an assorted cargo. Once her eight-man crew had been transferred to her captor, the *Gilfillan* was also burned.

It proved surprisingly easy to slip into Beaufort despite twenty-one shots from a blockading vessel, since they all went wide of their mark. Pegram responded with a single shot, refusing to waste powder because he knew himself to be out of range. About 7:00 A.M. on February 28 the *Nashville* was safely moored alongside the railroad wharf at Morehead City.

It was one thing to get safely into the port but an altogether different matter to get out again. All three channels leading to Beaufort Harbor were under constant surveillance by the Union warships *State of Georgia* and *Cambridge,* the gunboat *Chippewa,* and the bark *Gemsbok.* Any attempt to get past these vessels during daylight hours would be suicidal, Pegram decided. So he waited until the dark night of March 17, when he managed to escape at about 8:00 P.M. Four weeks later the Confederate warship eluded blockading ships and slipped into heavily guarded Wilmington, North Carolina. There Pegram seems to have taken on a full cargo before again passing through the blockade. Outward bound, the *Nashville* was flying English colors and temporarily bore the name *William L. Wragg.*

Indignant officials in Washington held two courts of inquiry about the so-called Wilmington affair. The commanders of the *Mount Vernon, State of Georgia, Penobscot,* and *Chippewa* informed Secretary Welles that they knew nothing about the escape. Yet a June court of inquiry ruled that Comdr. Charles Green of the USS *Jamestown* was "censurable for not having destroyed or attempted to destroy the supposed steamer *Nashville.*"

Meanwhile, leaving behind the confusion he had caused in North Carolina waters, Pegram sailed for the safety of Georgia's Great Ogeechee River, which was shielded from Union warships by Fort McAllister. Once there, however, he found he could not leave. Numer-

John Worden had commanded the USS *Monitor* against the CSS *Virginia.* Although the original Union ironclad was lost in a gale off North Carolina, Worden went on to command another ironclad, the *Montauk,* in the South Atlantic Blockading Squadron and destroyed the CSS *Nashville* while engaged in operations around Fort McAllister.

ous Federal vessels were stationed nearby, and their commanders maintained a twenty-four-hour watch.

Pegram was given command of another vessel, and he waited patiently for eight months. He found solace in the certainty that although he could not get out of the river, Federal vessels could not get into it. A line of torpedoes across its mouth was designed to stop light vessels, and the guns of Fort McAllister would deter any attack.

Comdr. John L. Worden of the Union ironclad *Montauk* was made of especially stern stuff, however. Late in February 1863, he was handed a report saying that the *Nashville* had been seen in motion above Fort McAllister. Worden immediately sent out a reconnaissance party, which found that the famous little ship had run aground.

The Federal commander calculated that he could get within range of his quarry without exposing his vessel to Fort McAllister. Thus he moved up the river at daylight on February 27, accompanied by the *Seneca, Wissahickon,* and the gunboat *Dawn.*

Under fire from shore, the *Montauk* moved within twelve hundred yards of the *Nashville,* whose timbers could be seen above an intervening wooded islet. Paymaster Samuel T. Browne recorded that the *Montauk* anchored at 7:04. At 7:07 the warship fired one shot to see if it had the range to hit the *Nashville.* Satisfied with that, the small flotilla opened a barrage against the lone Confederate vessel, which continued for almost an hour. At 8:13 dense fog set in and did not lift until 8:40. When it cleared, lookouts reported that the *Nashville* was afire from stem to stern and the vessel's smokestack had fallen. By 9:05 the *Nashville* was a blazing hulk. Half an hour later her magazine exploded and shattered what was left of the warship that had made headlines in London and New York.

Although she went down with only one cruise to her credit, the CSS *Nashville* had sent shock waves throughout the North. Her raid in the English Channel failed in its chief purpose, but it created near panic in Yankee financial circles. A passenger ship running between New York and Charleston before the outbreak of hostilities, the *Nashville* was the only side-wheeler converted into a warship that made headlines throughout the Western world.

Newspaper tributes to the ship and her crew may have had some impact upon public opinion in England and on the Continent. Far more importantly, say some naval historians, the voyage led to foreign recognition of Confederate warships as bona fide belligerents. To the lasting chagrin of Charles F. Adams—son and grandson of two U.S. presidents—it also led England to demonstrate that such a vessel could find safety in a neutral port.

22

Jeb Stuart

One Hundred Thousand Blue Monkeys

At Dabb's Farm, Virginia, on the morning of June 11, 1862, Gen. Robert E. Lee conferred at length with his cavalry commander, Brig. Gen. James Ewell Brown "Jeb" Stuart. A written summary of his orders stated in part: "You are desired to make a secret movement to the rear of the enemy, now posted on the Chickahominy [River], with a view of gaining intelligence of his operations, communications, &c; of driving in his foraging parties, and securing such grain, cattle, &c, for ourselves as you can make arrangements to have driven in. Another object is to destroy his wagon trains, said to be passing daily from the Piping Tree Road to his camp on the Chickahominy."

Aware of Stuart's dashing character, Lee warned: "You will return as soon as the object of your expedition is accomplished, and you must bear constantly in mind, while endeavoring to execute the general purpose of your mission, not to hazard unnecessarily your command or to attempt what your judgment may not approve; but be content to accomplish all the good you can without feeling it necessary to obtain all that might be desired." Deliberately veiled, Lee's admonition took on new meaning five days later when Stuart and 1,199 of his 1,200 picked men returned from an expedition with no exact parallel in Civil War annals.

Maj. Gen. George B. McClellan was humiliated by Stuart's uncontested ride around his one-hundred-thousand-man army, but his soldiers were not endangered.

A story goes that Cpl. Turner Doswell was grinning from ear to ear when he rejoined his comrades on June 16. Having been reared just north of Richmond, he served as one of Stuart's scouts and reputedly summarized their foray as having "turned [Gen. George A.] McClellan's 100,000 soldiers into monkeys in blue."

For his secret excursion deep into enemy territory, Stuart picked three cavalry units and a section of horse artillery. Significantly, two of his three top subordinates in the special brigade were closely related to his commander. Col. W. H. F. "Rooney" Lee of the Ninth Virginia Cavalry was the son of Robert E. Lee, and Col. Fitzhugh Lee of the First Virginia Cavalry was his cousin. Col. William T. Martin led the third unit, made up of 250 picked men from the Jeff Davis Legion of cavalry.

Not even these colonels knew their mission or where they were going until Stuart roused them on June 12, about two hours after midnight. Warning against the customary use of bugles, which might be heard by the enemy, the commanders and their men moved northward from their base near Yellow Tavern. Riding just east of the Richmond and Fredericksburg Railroad, they turned toward Hanover Court House as they approached the South Anna River.

Near Gibson's Mill, trees and underbrush slowed their progress and concealed a small body of blue-clad soldiers. As soon as the Union troops were spotted, Confederate Capt. William Latane raised his saber, shouted to his squadron to follow him, and raced toward the enemy at a gallop. Prussian-born Heros von Borcke, who was riding beside Latane, later reported that just as the Federals rushed into the road, Latane "fell from his horse, shot dead." After a series of hand-to-hand combats, however, the members of McClellan's cavalry squadron who survived were thrown into full retreat.

Near the point of this brief but fierce struggle, said von Borcke, farmers and their wives flocked to greet the Confederate riders. Several of them brought fresh food, and a few had flowers in their hands. One bouquet was handed to Stuart, who gallantly vowed to preserve it and take it into Richmond.

Riding toward the east, the men, who still did not know their destination, turned south at Putney's Ferry and soon reached the Richmond and York River Railway. Since Robert E. Lee was known to be especially sensitive about possible troop movements by rail, von Borck's report stressed his personal efforts to obstruct the railroad track at Tunstall's Station. In addition to felling a big tree so that it dropped across the tracks, he placed on them "an oak sill about a foot square and fourteen feet long."

Von Borck could have saved himself and his men their efforts. When a train came thundering down the track, the locomotive easily knocked the obstructions aside. According to the Prussian, Stuart's riders then "threw in a close and effective fire upon the passing train." This resulted in numerous Federal casualties he said, but that report was never confirmed.

Pursuing his journey southward, Stuart ran into serious trouble when he reached the Chickahominy River. Swollen by heavy spring rains, it had overflowed its banks, and water was two feet deep for a distance of half a mile from the stream. Efforts to swim the horses over the river proved futile; during two hours, only about seventy-five animals and their riders made the crossing. Stuart then personally scouted the region and discovered the supports of a bridge that had been burned. Dismantling an abandoned warehouse, the Confederates built a narrow foot bridge and soon inched gingerly across, holding the bridles of their horses that had to swim alongside the shaky bridge.

Once across the river, the Confederates headed toward Charles City Court House. When they reached it, asserted von Borcke, no man in the expedition "had closed his eyes in sleep for forty-eight hours." Veteran cavalrymen knew how to sleep in the saddle, and each night Stuart's men usually were allowed to stop for a three-hour rest, so the Prussian's comment may have been an exaggeration.

Under a full moon, the gray-clad riders had turned toward the northwest and Richmond when scouts came in sight of the James River. To reach their capital, the Southerners had to cover thirty miles through territory believed to be firmly in the grip of their enemies. Escorted only by a scout and a courier, Stuart stayed in the saddle all night and reached Lee's headquarters before first light on June 15. Members of his expedition straggled in during the next eight or ten hours. Pvts. J. A. Timberlake and R. E. Frayser, who knew the country and stayed ahead of Stuart's column, compared notes and agreed that they had ridden about a hundred miles since their departure.

The Confederates lost only one of their number—Latane—and reported having killed or captured about two hundred men in blue. Numerous Federal wagons were burned, along with two small schooners, and scores of horses were captured. Several dozen of Stuart's followers were especially elated; they were the lucky ones who took a Federal ordnance wagon and then helped themselves to canteens and Colt revolvers.

The information that Lee wanted about the location of McClellan's forces was provided, which guided him in making decisions that led to the Seven Days' campaign. The most important aspect of the three days of incessant riding, however, was the impact it had on morale in the South and in the North. Incredibly, Stuart had led his men around the entire Federal army and had lost only one man.

Confederates everywhere gloated that "Beauty," as Stuart was called because he wore colorful and expensive uniforms, had "demonstrated that one Rebel is worth half a dozen Yanks six days a week and a full dozen on Sunday!" Throughout the North, recruitment centers were woefully empty for several weeks after news of Stuart's ride circulated.

In his official report Stuart alluded to his conversation with Lee during which he broached the idea of making a great splash by riding around the entire Federal force that menaced Richmond. It was this grandiose idea that had prompted Lee to warn Stuart not to engage in hastily considered moves.

Although the military impact of the successful expedition was not significant, the man who planned and led it received several rewards. Clearly he had won the respect of Robert E. Lee. That was of great

LIBRARY OF CONGRESS

His dashing appearance plus his choice of sprightly horses caused Stuart's admirers to call him "Beauty."

importance, since Lee had not assumed the post of commander of what he named the Army of Northern Virginia until June 1, succeeding Joseph E. Johnston, who had been wounded at Seven Pines in May.

An outpouring of adulation by both soldiers and civilians constituted a second reward for Stuart. Far more than most daring and successful leaders, the native of Virginia's Patrick County seemed actually to need praise. When he received none for a period of months, he was likely to become morose and sullen. After having made monkeys of the entire Federal Department of Virginia, he was affable and expansive.

A third source of great satisfaction was intensely personal. He had quarreled with his father-in-law over the question of states' rights and secession, and the two had become enemies. Hence Stuart gloated at having defeated a cavalry force commanded by his wife's father, Brig. Gen. Philip St. George Cooke, a thirty-nine-year veteran of U.S. Army service.

Some evidence supports the conclusion that the rewards he reaped from his famous ride went to the head of Jeb Stuart. Having "done the absolutely impossible" once, he seems to have reasoned, Why not do it again . . . and again?

With or without permission from his superiors, Stuart planned and executed a second ride around most of McClellan's forces in October 1862. Then the cavalry leader who craved adulation once more launched a ride around Federal forces late in June 1863. The third time his scheme backfired. Although he nearly succeeded in encircling the enemy forces, it caused him to be absent when the battle of Gettysburg commenced. Had he failed in June or in October 1862, Stuart might not have made his 1863 try. Because he and his men were busy riding around tens of thousands of soldiers in blue, he could not provide Lee with badly needed intelligence during the early hours of the biggest battle of the war.

Since his years as a cadet at West Point, Beauty Stuart had been reasonably well acquainted with great literature of the English language. Hence his third ride may have led him to remember and to meditate upon lines from John Dryden's *Don Sebastian:*

> O the curst fate of all conspiracies!
> They move on many springs; if one but fail
> The restive machine stops.

23

Ulysses S. Grant

The River Bypass

SITTING ON THE GROUND, leaning against a big poplar tree, and whittling in a slow but methodical fashion, Maj. Gen. Ulysses S. Grant pondered his next move. "River rats" among his command had spent most of their lives on the Mississippi and its tributaries. According to them, as recently as a decade earlier there had been a bypass that enabled boats to leave the great river and then reenter it many miles to the south.

Not far below Helena, Arkansas, he was told, on the opposite shore, an old bed of the Mississippi once connected it with Moon Lake. Called the Yazoo Pass, it allowed shallow-draft boats to enter the lake, then followed the Coldwater and Tallahatchie Rivers to the Yazoo, which emptied into the Mississippi just above Vicksburg. This was an ideal back door to Vicksburg if Grant could get into Yazoo Pass, which the state of Mississippi had blocked by a levee in 1858 to curtail annual floods.

Confederate batteries on the high bluffs overlooking Vicksburg literally commanded that stretch of the Mississippi. To take "the Gibraltar of the South," Grant could not use a frontal attack.

The inventive Grant had already tried and failed twice to circumvent Vicksburg. First, he tried to redirect the Mississippi away from Vicksburg by way of a canal. Second, he tried to devise an alternate

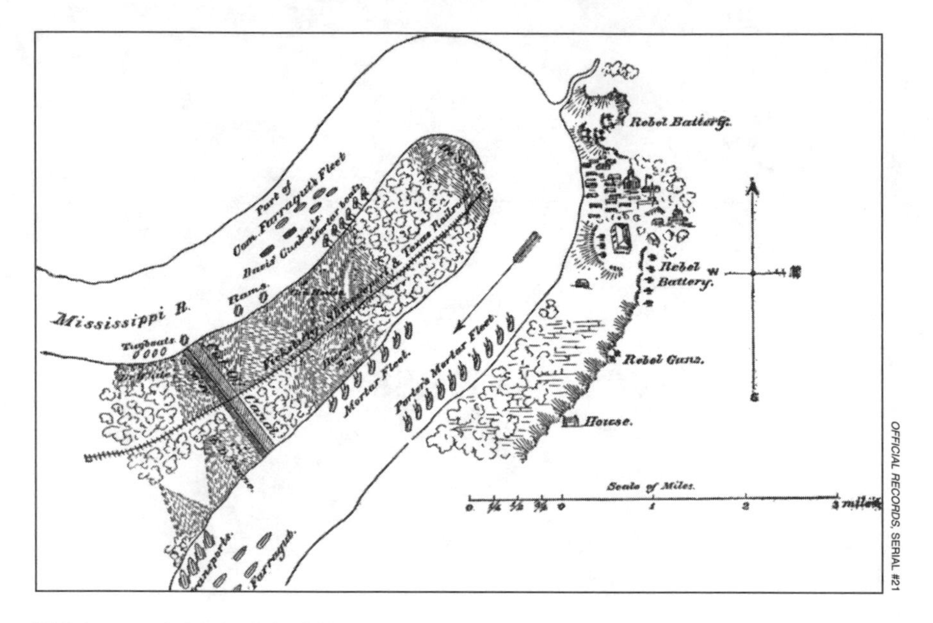

OFFICIAL RECORDS, SERIAL #21

Vicksburg and vicinity, July 1862.

route through the Tensas, Washita, Black, and Red Rivers to bypass Vicksburg, but the terrain was mostly swampland and hardly suitable for maneuvering an army.

The tenacious Grant would not give up, so the Yazoo Pass expedition was launched. For it to succeed, military and naval forces would have to be coordinated. Such an effort seemed highly promising on February 4, 1863, when Acting Master George W. Brown of the Union gunboat *Forest Rose* made his first report to Rear Adm. David D. Porter. "The levee is cut," he wrote, "and the water is gushing through at a terrible rate." So rapid was the current that it swept away "old logs, trees, and everything in its way" and formed a channel about seventy-five yards wide.

Lt. Col. James H. Wilson of Grant's staff helped to plan and execute the destruction of the levee. On February 7 he dispatched a cheerful summary of events since his arrival five days earlier. "Today," he gloated, "the first steamboat swept through and launched its exploration of the river beyond."

Aboard the USS *Rattler,* Lt. Comdr. Watson Smith directed the gunboats *Chillicothe, Baron De Kalb, Marmora, Romeo,* and *Forest Rose* and

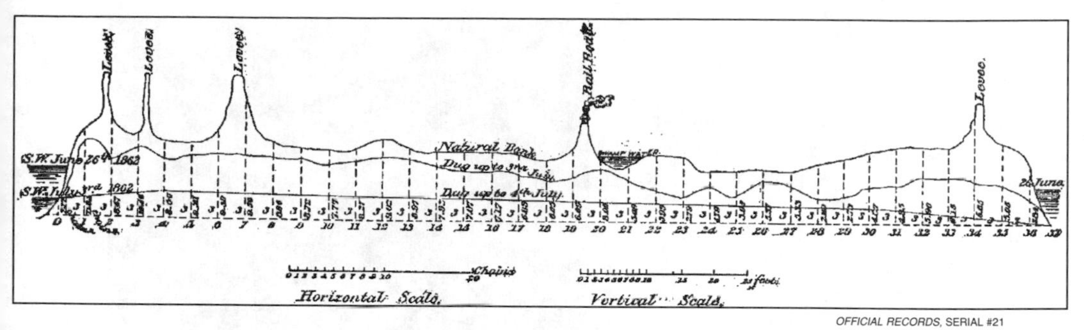

OFFICIAL RECORDS, SERIAL #21

A novel approach to the Vicksburg siege was suggested by President Lincoln: divert the river away from the town by digging a canal across Burey's Point, opposite the town. It was carefully planned and vigorously executed—but failed.

the side-wheel towboat *S. Bayard.* With three barges of coal in tow, Smith was eager for the arrival of transports bearing soldiers.

Moon Lake was entered without incident, and the flotilla moved forward about five miles in just one hour. On February 28 the Federal vessels reached the Coldwater River, where their progress was more rapid. Smith expected to burn railroad bridges, which would impede Confederate troop movements, and to find and destroy some unfinished enemy gunboats.

Long before he was near such targets, his boats were badly damaged by increasingly dense clumps of big trees. Smokestacks tumbled to the decks when they encountered overhanging limbs, and the vessels' hulls were punctured by underwater obstacles. Wilson, who was in charge of the army engineers responsible for clearing the channels, found many immense trees lying across the river. Sometimes he had to put two regiments on a single cable to remove a forest giant from the water with hawsers.

Brig. Gen. Leonard F. Ross, head of the military phase of the movement, commanded a forty-five-hundred-man brigade made up of nine regiments of infantry and one light field battery. Crowded upon twenty-two shallow-draft transports, they moved along the course selected by Grant as rapidly as possible. On good days they proceeded at least one mile.

Artillery in the army division might be needed. Scouts reported that the Confederates were hastily erecting a line of fortifications from cotton bales and sandbags, which they called by the grandiose name of Fort Pemberton. It was on a narrow neck of land north of the town

U. S. Grant was determined to take Vicksburg. It was the turning point of his career.

of Greenwood where the Yalobusha and Tallahatchie Rivers joined to form the Yazoo. Breaking the Mississippi River levee to open the way into Moon Lake had caused a mammoth flood in the region, so Fort Pemberton was in effect on an island unapproachable from upstream. Once in the Yazoo, however, the Federals could move easily and rapidly into the Mississippi. Soon they and their divisions that followed them could reach Vicksburg's northern approaches from the rear and score a glorious victory.

At his headquarters Grant was so elated that some of his officers wondered whether he had been drinking again. He dispelled that notion by preparing detailed orders for a second division to move to support Ross. He then notified Maj. Gen. James B. McPherson that his entire Seventeenth Corps would be expected to moved toward Snyder's Bluff as soon as Yazoo Pass was open.

On March 11 the *Chillicothe* steamed toward Fort Pemberton and opened fire, expecting to reduce it quickly. Instead, the 395-ton side-wheel steamer was found to be woefully unprepared for battle.

Hit repeatedly, the vessel's walls of nine-inch white pine proved too thin. The buckling of her walls caused the bolts holding her iron skin in place to give way, "causing great destruction." Gunners were aghast when they saw that a shot was headed toward an eleven-inch shell they were trying to load. Hasty flight proved futile; the Confederate projectile entered a partly opened port, and its impact caused both shells to explode with such force that eighteen hundred-pound port covers were tossed overboard. The crew suffered fourteen casualties as a result of that one shot.

Smith ordered his ironclad to withdraw so "its powers of endurance could be increased by using well-pressed bales of cotton to shield it." For four days occasional forays by gunboats and attempts by infantry to take Fort Pemberton failed to dislodge the enemy. Disheartened and disgusted, leaders of the joint expedition agreed that it was useless to proceed.

General Ross roared that gunboats which should have advanced at dawn did not get under way until 7:00 or 7:30 and habitually "stopped and lay to an hour for dinner." According to the commander of the division, soldiers and a few marines would have reached and passed the island before the Rebel guns could have been mounted, had the steamers not moved so leisurely.

Lieutenant Commander Smith was so devastated that he took to a sickbed and relegated his post to Lt. Comdr. James P. Foster. Foster's official report to Porter ended by charging that failure was due to the fact that "the army detained us by the slowness of their movements."

Charges and countercharges did nothing to soothe Grant, for the heart of the matter was that his grand scheme had failed. Now he would have to devise an entirely different way to take Vicksburg.

24

Alexander H. Stephens

No Peace But a Union Peace

ALTHOUGH HE WAS AFFECTIONATELY known as "Little Alec" because of his diminutive size, there was nothing small about the mind of Alexander H. Stephens. An admiring colleague said he had "an awesome gift conferred . . . upon the man from Crawfordsville by the Almighty."

Admitted to the bar at age twenty-two, the Georgia native entered politics, went to the U.S. House of Representatives for sixteen years, and became nationally lauded as "the Great Commoner." In the crucial election of 1860 he supported Stephen A. Douglas and warned his fellow Democrats that a split in their party would guarantee the election of the Republican nominee, regardless of who that might be.

Many South Carolina leaders were wanting to secede from the Union and might have done so regardless of which Republican was elected because the new Republican Party was on record as opposed to slavery. Although he was moderate on the slavery question, Abraham Lincoln was denounced as being one of a coterie of "Black Republicans." After his election, South Carolina severed its ties with the Union on December 20, 1860.

Close to the Palmetto State both geographically and ideologically, Georgia showed early signs of being ready to secede. In this climate Stephens was among the minority that objected to pulling out of the

HARPER'S WEEKLY

Once when both Lincoln and Alexander Stephens were congressmen, the diminutive Stephens delivered an oration on the floor that reputedly moved Lincoln to tears.

Union. Far better, he urged, to remain in the United States and try to thwart the Republican administration from the inside.

His fellow citizens paid little attention to the man whom many admired and most respected. By an overwhelming margin, their representatives voted for secession on January 19, 1861, and the city of Savannah indulged in an all-night celebration.

Like many other southerners, Stephens put loyalty to his state above his personal views. Hence he accepted a place in the delegation sent by Georgia to the Provisional Congress of the not-yet-established Confederate States of America. To his surprise, in Montgomery, Alabama, he was unanimously chosen as vice president of the new nation. Since its constitution was largely adapted from the Constitution of the United States, that meant he would preside over sessions of the Confederate Senate.

In April 1861 he allayed some of the fears that had been voiced that he could not get along with the new president, Jefferson Davis. Stephens declared himself "to be in happy accord" with a statement of purpose issued by Davis that was offered as a summary of Confederate goals: "We seek no conquest, no aggrandizement, no concessions from the free States. All we ask is to be let alone—that none shall attempt our subjugation by arms. This we will and must resist to the direst extremity. The moment this pretention is abandoned the sword will

GEORGIA HISTORICAL SOCIETY

Savannah, then Georgia's largest city, indulged in an orgy of celebration when the state's secession was announced January 19, 1861.

drop from our hands, and we shall be ready to enter into treaties of amity and commerce [that will prove to be] mutually beneficial."

A competent scholar of the U.S. Constitution, Stephens denounced the "war measures" of Lincoln as without legal foundation. Once Federal troops invaded Virginia, he declared that their actions constituted "an unjust war aimed at conquest and subjugation, with full responsibility for all sacrifices of blood and treasure resting upon the Washington administration." Although neither man was fully aware of it, both Stephens and Lincoln were strongly influenced by the writings of Thomas Jefferson.

Adopting the Jeffersonian view that state governments should be strong and the central government relatively weak, Stephens soon found himself at odds with Davis, who repeatedly tried to strengthen power in Richmond. As a result, Stephens opposed numerous Confederate war measures, but he tried to avoid public condemnation of them by spending as little time as possible in the Southern capital.

By the summer of 1863 it was well known that he was an outspoken proponent of any measure that would reduce the slaughter on the battlefields. He and Lincoln had developed a mutual admiration when both of them were members of Congress; if any Southerner could meet the U.S. president on nearly equal terms, it was Stephens.

One of the big issues of 1863 was the end of the exchanging of prisoners of war, a practice halted largely through the influence of Lt. Gen. U. S. Grant, who argued that allowing men to return home helped the South, which suffered a manpower shortage. They would immediately reenlist to fight again. Stephens suggested a meeting with Lincoln to negotiate a return to the former policy. Davis assented to the suggestion readily, almost eagerly. Then and now, some critics of the Confederate head of state have cited evidence they believe proves Davis expected and wanted a conspicuous failure by the man first in line to succeed him. That verdict may or may not be correct. Whatever Davis's motives may have been in agreeing to the Stephens proposal, the vice president's trip to the Federal capital accomplished nothing.

Soon thereafter the statesman from Georgia became an outspoken proponent of peace at almost any price. He may have harbored these views for months before making them public, but he seems to have spoken out during the summer of 1864 because he sensed mounting support for peace in both the South and the North. Lincoln's July 18 call for an additional half-million fighting men helped to set the stage for a series of events.

Horace Greeley, founder and editor of the most widely circulated newspaper in North America, let it be known that he was willing to try to persuade military leaders on both sides to order a cease-fire. He called for like-minded persons to meet with him at Niagara Falls and went there with high hopes. Since nothing came of his effort, he was ridiculed.

In both the North and the South, many peace advocates found it dangerous to air their views in public. Long before Greeley's humiliation, another proponent of peace found himself in serious trouble. Clement L. Vallandigham of Ohio, once regarded as a potential presidential candidate, was arrested in the middle of the night and jailed as a traitor. Perhaps because he was unwilling to face the public reaction to a long prison sentence for Vallandigham, Lincoln banished the peace advocate to Confederate territory. Transported to Tennessee, the Ohio politician remained there only briefly before taking refuge in Canada.

A shift in public opinion, however, occurred in 1864. Writing to his wife on August 29, Confederate Brig. Gen. Stephen D. Ramseur echoed sentiments that were widely held. To his beloved Ellen, he said, "I am growing more hopeful about the ending of the War. Every person whose views I have requested, and who has had an opportunity to learn the feeling of Yankee civilians and soldiers, assures me that the north is tired of war and will choose an out-and-out peace man during the presidential election in November."

George Brinton McClellan would have rejoiced had he read Ramseur's letter. Nominated for the presidency by the Democratic Party with an antiwar platform, McClellan was confident he would win. His opponent, Abraham Lincoln, appealed to voters to do whatever might be necessary to preserve the Union.

During the fall, Maj. Gen. William T. Sherman's capture of Atlanta and Maj. Gen. Philip Sheridan's successful Shenandoah Valley campaign vindicated Lincoln's firm war policy. McClellan carried only three states, with 12 electoral votes compared to Lincoln's 212.

Now Stephens concocted what has been called "the most audacious scheme of the Civil War." Given a free hand, the Confederate vice president planned to make the most of his ties with Lincoln. If authorized by Davis, he would again travel through the military lines to Washington to seek a truce leading to a formal armistice.

The scheme appeared to be feasible and the timing ideal. The Confederate situation was desperate. Its troops were dangerously short of weapons, shoes, ammunition, and supplies. Lincoln's adviser, Francis P. Blair, had put his influence behind Northern efforts to stop the shooting. Lincoln was known to have floated a proposal under whose terms 10 percent of voters in a seceded state could take the oath of allegiance, form a new government, and be readmitted to the Union.

Despite these favorable omens, no one was more aware of the mission's dangers than was Stephens; failure could make him a laughingstock on both sides and bring an end to his political career. Nationally famous spokesmen such as the Reverend Henry Ward Beecher had gone on record as being "fearful that Lincoln would be anxious for peace" and afraid that "he would accept something that would be of advantage to the South."

Davis quickly selected a pair of experienced politicians to accompany the vice president. Robert Hunter of Virginia, a Confederate senator, had spent six years in the U.S. House of Representatives, fourteen in the U.S. Senate, and served briefly as Confederate secretary of state. Judge John A. Campbell had been an associate justice of the U.S. Supreme Court from the Franklin Pierce administration until two weeks after the artillery duel at Fort Sumter. He had many close ties with key members of the Lincoln administration, including the secretary of state, William H. Seward. In written instructions to the trio,

FRANK LESLIE'S ILLUSTRATED NEWSPAPER

When Francis P. Blair Sr. tried to mediate peace, he was derided as being "a granny woman."

Davis stipulated, "You are to proceed to Washington City for an informal conference with [Lincoln] upon the issues involved in the existing war, and for the purpose of securing peace to the two countries."

An exchange of telegrams on January 29 culminated in Lincoln's declaration to the public that he knew of "no commission and no negotiations." By this he may have meant that he did not regard Stephens and his companions as representing a legitimate government. The Northern president seemed to have planned initially to delegate the work to a subordinate.

Expecting safe passage to the Federal capital, the Southerners were instructed instead to proceed to Hampton Roads, Virginia. Passing through Federal lines under the command of Maj. Gen. Edward O. Ord, they were shunted to Grant's headquarters for a brief stay. On February 3, 1865, aboard the steamer *River Queen,* the three commissioners came face to face with Lincoln and his secretary of state, who had traveled by way of Fort Monroe. Having stipulated that no written memoranda would be made and no aides would be present, the only records of the momentous parlay are statements made afterward by its participants. Newspaper accounts were dismissed by Stephens as "utterly unworthy of notice."

Stephens seems to have opened the discussion by asking Lincoln whether there was any way to bring the slaughter to a halt. According to Stephens's later written account, the president nodded and said

Not long after the unsuccessful Hampton Roads conference with Stephens, Lincoln met with Grant, Sherman, and Porter to plot the concluding strategy of the war.

that fighting would cease the moment all resistance to the laws of the Union ended.

Although talks continued for two or three hours, negotiations effectively ended with this initial statement by Lincoln. When the five leaders parted company, all of them knew that he would never agree to an armistice. Peace, he had made it clear, would come only after the unconditional surrender of all Rebel forces.

Disappointed, the Confederate vice president spent only a few hours in Richmond before retiring to Georgia. On the long trip home, he may have wondered what Davis had hoped to achieve by seeming to be enthusiastic about the scheme for peace. Postwar evidence indicates that the Confederate president was sure that Federal terms would prove unacceptable before he selected Hunter and Campbell to go with Stephens.

Imprisoned after the war, Stephens and Davis had a brief meeting before Stephens was dispatched to Fort Warren at Boston. They never met again. No one knows what the Confederate president thought of his vice president's scheme. Neither does anyone know precisely what took place aboard the *River Queen* at Hampton Roads.

Politically, Davis had the Union demands widely published, steeling Southern resolve to continue the fight and temporarily squelching all defeatist talk. Lincoln, however, had tipped his hand regarding a beneficent Reconstruction and caused an uproar in the ranks of the Republican Party. The resulting polarization of the party leadership in Congress led to a firm entrenchment of Radical Republican ideas and a resolve to impose punitive measures against the South when the war was over.

25

Robert C. Kennedy

The Fiery Plans of Southern Terrorism

If THE STORY IS true, it was one of the most insidious schemes concocted by one of the most elusive figures of the Civil War. The story begins with the confession filed by Lt. Col. Martin Burke and submitted to Maj. Gen. John A. Dix, commander of the military Department of the East, which was headquartered in New York City. The prisoner was named Robert C. Kennedy, and he admitted the following:

Fort Lafayette March 25, 1865

> After my escape from Johnson's Island I went to Canada, where I met a number of Confederates. They asked me if I was willing to go on an expedition. I replied, "Yes, if it is in the service of my country." They said, "It's all right," but gave no intimation of its nature, nor did I ask for any. I was then sent to New York, where I staid [*sic*] for some time. There were eight men in our party, two of whom fled to Canada. After we had been in New York three weeks, we were told that the object of the expedition was to retaliate on the North for . . . Sheridan's atrocities in the Shenandoah Valley. [W]e desired to destroy property, not the lives of women and children, although that of course would have followed in its train.

Little is known about Kennedy, but he is believed to have been a native of Georgia who volunteered for service in a Confederate regiment raised in New Orleans. By the fall of 1863 he was a twenty-seven-year-old captain on the headquarters staff of Maj. Gen. Joseph Wheeler, who was then engaged in a series of raids in Tennessee.

On October 12 Kennedy was ordered to Chattanooga and charged with the tasks of securing supplies and delivering messages to Confederate leaders in and around Chattanooga. Somewhere on his journey Kennedy was captured. He was sent to Ohio's most notorious prison, Johnson's Island near Sandusky, and nearly a year after his capture he escaped to Canada.

Soon after having crossed the border, the fugitive learned from other refugees that Jacob Thompson was recruiting men for special missions. As the chief Confederate agent in Canada, Thompson regularly received substantial sums of money from Richmond. Working with another agent appointed by Jefferson Davis, Clement C. Clay, Thompson spent freely on what the Confederate Secret Service designated only as "special undertakings" and was never rebuked for doing so.

A special remittance of fifty thousand dollars from Richmond reached Canada in August 1864 and was immediately deposited in a joint bank account held by Thompson and Clay. According to information later developed by the U.S. judge advocate general, Joseph Holt, the pair initially planned for Kennedy to play a leading role in the Northwest Conspiracy. For reasons never clarified, they soon told the fugitive that he would lead an expedition to New York City. Considerable evidence indicates that the Confederate Signal Corps, headed by Maj. William Norris, was ordered to assist in the plot.

Convinced that President Davis had given his personal assent to the scheme developed by Clay, Holt reported that the chief objective of the conspirators was to torch the city of New York. Later denounced by Federal authorities as "one of the greatest atrocities of the age," the conflagration was initially planned for election night, November 8, 1864.

Lt. Col. Robert M. Martin is sometimes identified as having commanded the New York raiders. Although he was almost certainly a member of the band, Martin's role was less important than that of Kennedy.

During the first week of October, Kennedy and Martin reached their objective without being challenged. Soon at least six other conspirators joined them. One man was not identified in surviving

In 1860 Wall Street was regarded as the financial hub of the nation.

documents, but the names of Emile Longuemare, John W. Headley, John T. Ashbrook, James T. Herrington, John M. Price, and James Chenault appear with regularity.

Six days before the target date, the U.S. secretary of state, William H. Seward, learned of the plan from an informer. He directed Maj. Gen. Benjamin F. Butler to take charge of protecting the city.

When Butler arrived with troops numbering between thirty-five hundred and six thousand, Kennedy and his fellow conspirators panicked. Deciding to let election night pass without action, they agreed among themselves they would have a better chance of success on Thanksgiving Day. On November 8, 1864, heavily Democratic New York City voted for former Maj. Gen. George B. McClellan, with Abraham Lincoln polling only about half as many votes as did his one-time field commander.

As time passed, at least two of the conspirators returned to their refuge in Canada. Late in the afternoon of November 25, the six remaining terrorists put the first phase of their plan into action. One of them, John Headley, later published a book-length, step-by-step account of their doings.

If Headley is to be believed—and he is the source of most of the information about the plot—each man was assigned multiple targets.

NATIONAL ARCHIVES

No one saw conspirators at work, hence newspaper artists relied upon their imagination.

According to Kennedy's confession, he was assigned Barnum's Museum, Lovejoy's Hotel, the Tammany Hotel, and the New England House. He apparently checked into all three hotels well before dark, using a different name at each. Hotels assigned to Headley were the Astor, the City, and the United States. Martin was responsible for the Saint Denis Hotel, the Hoffman House, and the Fifth Avenue Hotel. Ashbrook was given what targets were left in the heart of the city: the Saint James, the LaFarge, and the Saint Nicholas Hotels. Initial plans seem to have called for the seizure of the U.S. subtreasury building and Fort Lafayette, but the conspirators decided that they were too few in number to execute this phase of the plot.

Kennedy or Longuemare or both had earlier made contact with a Confederate chemist who had fled to New York. They paid him an undisclosed sum to generate 144 four-ounce bottles of a substance popularly known as Greek fire. Two of its active ingredients, phosphorus and hydrogen sulfide, caused it to flare at the touch of a lighted candle and burn with intense heat.

During the evening of November 24 and the morning of November 25, his handiwork was parceled out among the conspirators. Most of them received eighteen bottles, but since Kennedy's assignments also included the museum, he may have taken some that Ashbrook and Martin expected to receive.

Each participant then returned to the room he had booked in each hotel, splashed Greek fire on the bed and furniture, and when flames began to dart upward, dashed out locking the door behind him. Although Greek fire was known to be unreliable, 144 bottles of the compound could have turned the heart of the city into a raging inferno. As it was, the only hotel destroyed was the Saint Nicholas. At the Astor, the Metropolitan, and the Belmont, damage was confined to a few rooms or a single floor. Flames did not level the crowded Barnum's Museum, but they created pandemonium when the elephants, lions, and tigers took fright upon smelling the smoke.

Later called "the most extensive espionage expedition of 1861–65," the effort to reduce New York City to ashes was a miserable failure. Before midnight on November 25, special editions of the city's newspapers hit the streets with accounts of the fiasco. Worse for the Rebels who botched their job, several of them were identified by name in these early accounts.

Thoroughly frightened, most of the conspirators were gone before morning. One newspaper report said that all of them had "lit a rag for Canada" as soon as they realized that they were in danger of being arrested. That report was less than accurate. Kennedy was arrested in Detroit and returned to New York.

Brig. Gen. Fitz-Henry Warren headed an investigation of the incident. Meeting at Fort Lafayette in New York Harbor, members of this body convened on January 17, 1865, but did not announce their verdict until March 20.

CENTURY MAGAZINE

Judge Advocate General Joseph Holt

Kennedy was found guilty of having acted as a spy and of having violated the laws of war. "There is nothing in the annals of barbarism which evinces greater vindictiveness" than his actions, their report stated. It also said in part:

> It was not a mere attempt to destroy the city, but to set fire to crowded hotels and places of public resort. The evidence shows that Barnum's Museum and ten hotels were fired . . . indicating a cool calculation to create so many conflagrations at the same time as to baffle the efforts of the fire department to extinguish them. In all the buildings fired, not only noncombatant men, but women and children, were congregated in great numbers, and nothing but the most diabolical spirit of revenge could have impelled the incendiaries to act so revoltingly.

Sentenced to be hanged, Kennedy died shortly after noon on March 25. The hangman's noose should have put an end to speculation about his activities as a secret agent, but it did not.

After Lincoln's assassination, Federal authorities engaged in a widespread hunt for conspirators. The judge advocate general, Joseph Holt, seems to have concluded that "a Mr. Purcell of Virginia," whose first name he did not know, was the mastermind of the plot to which John Wilkes Booth was central. Purcell's destruction of "the great hydra," or assassination of Lincoln, said the judge advocate general, was expected to result in causing him to be "honored as the Hercules of the age."

Agents sent by Holt visited major Canadian cities and interviewed persons who claimed to have knowledge of the conspiracy that culminated in Lincoln's death on Good Friday 1865. These witnesses helped to lay the foundation for a still ongoing quest for the truth about the Booth conspiracy. Clay and Kennedy, said "eight reliable witnesses," were guiding spirits in the plot not only to do away with Lincoln but simultaneously to kill the members of his cabinet and U. S. Grant.

Holt eventually felt that he had secured "the chain of testimony" according to which the assassination of Lincoln "is fixed beyond reasonable doubt upon these two conspirators [Purcell and Kennedy]." With Kennedy already dead and Purcell nowhere to be found, he urged that Clay and former Confederate President Davis "be arraigned and tried before a military commission."

Even in the heated climate that followed the assassination, relatively few persons of influence accepted Holt's conclusion that Kennedy was the mastermind behind the plan to do away with seven cabinet members, Grant, and Lincoln. Nevertheless, by publicizing his views, Holt planted doubt that continues to sprout more than one hundred years after Kennedy took his secrets with him to the grave.

Part 6

Flood Tide of Fraternal Strife

HARPER'S WEEKLY

Confederate President Jefferson Davis was a former U.S. senator and secretary of war.

26

Jefferson Davis

Citizen Pirates

TELEGRAPH OFFICES OF THE South became busy as soon as Abraham Lincoln announced his call for seventy-five thousand volunteers on Monday, April 15, 1861. Word of the Federal action reached Montgomery, Alabama, soon after noon. Jefferson Davis, preparing for his inauguration as president of the Confederate States of America on Tuesday, hesitated for many minutes after receiving the news. After the gala inaugural ceremonies in the Alabama capitol, the Confederate chief executive retired to his temporary office and labored until nearly midnight.

On Wednesday, April 17, Davis revealed his retaliation for "having a vast army raised for the obvious purpose of invading the peace-seeking South." The Confederate president invited owners of suitable vessels to make application for letters of marque and reprisal to prey upon the North's ocean commerce. This was an old custom whereby governments at war granted commissions, or licenses, to private owners of ships, giving them authority to wage war against enemy shipping. Vessels sailing under such commissions were called privateers. American privateers had operated against the British in both the Revolutionary War and the War of 1812.

Since Lincoln branded the secessionist movement an insurrection, the United States never officially declared war on the Confederacy;

At Montgomery, Alabama, the Provisional Confederate Congress met to frame a constitution and elect leaders.

PICTORIAL HISTORY OF THE CONFEDERACY

however, on May 3, the Confederate Congress declared that a state of war existed between the United States of America and the Confederate States of America. Many in the South hailed this enthusiastically, partly because a rider endorsed the president's action concerning letters of marque and reprisal, which effectively unleashed the privateers.

Davis, a man who tried to hide his emotions, must have been silently gratified when he saw a copy of the May 12 issue of the *Mobile Advertiser* that trumpeted:

> Let patriotic citizens go forth upon the trackless war path of the ocean to fight for their country in the most effective manner. Hundreds and hundreds of millions of the property of the enemy [Yankee ships and their cargoes] invite them to spoil him—to "spoil these Egyptians" of the North, who would coerce us to staying when we strove peaceably to make our exodus to independence of their oppressive thrall. The richly laden ships of the enemy swarm on every sea, and are absolutely unprotected. The harvest is ripe; let it be gathered, and we will strike the enemy to the heart—for we hit his pocket, his most sensitive part. His treasure ships, laden with California wealth, traverse Southern waters. Let them be the prize of the bravest and most enterprising. His commerce is the very life of the enemy's solvency and financial vitality. Strike it, and you lay the axe to the root of his power—you

> rend away the sinews of war. It is easy to put privateers afloat. There are an abundance of brave men among us ready to volunteer to fight anywhere. In this privateering the most enormous returns are promised with but trifling risk. Let us scour the seas, and sweep their commerce from it with the besom of destruction.

On May 14 the *New Orleans Picayune* confided the following: "Already a capital privateering vessel has been fitted out in this city. It is now ready, fully armed and ably officered, waiting for the letters of marque and reprisal which are daily expected from Montgomery. The work of fitting out another privateer is going on, something over one-fourth of the stock of $200,000 having been subscribed up to the hour of the meeting at noon yesterday in the old United States Courtroom, for the purpose of furthering the enterprise."

The next day the same newspaper informed its readers: "Books were opened yesterday at the Merchants' Exchange for subscriptions to stock in a propeller steamer to be fitted out as a privateer. Fifty thousand dollars have already been subscribed, and fifty thousand more are required. A fine chance is now presented to our enterprising citizens to embark in a venture which cannot fail of yielding a handsome profit."

LIBRARY OF CONGRESS

Captured by privateers, the bark *Tacony* (right) was converted into a raider—here shown burning another vessel.

Reaction in Great Britain was not quite what Davis wanted or expected. On June 3 Lord John Russell announced in Parliament that Confederate privateers would not be permitted to bring their prizes (or captured vessels) into any British port. Concurrently, the Duke of Newcastle released a statement that stressed Queen Victoria's eagerness to "observe the strictest neutrality in the contest which appears to be imminent" in North America. The queen, said the nobleman, had decided to refuse to let privateers enter "into the ports, harbors, roadsteads, or waters of the United Kingdom, or any of Her Majesty's colonies or possessions abroad."

This news from abroad did not reach North America until weeks after enterprising Confederate investors and sailors had begun to act. Early in April the crew of the U.S. revenue cutter *Aiken* had assembled on a Charleston dock. Several had already notified their captain that it was time to decide. Not simply willing, but eager, he had made arrangements to take a vote.

"Every man who wants to continue to serve Washington say 'Aye,'" he directed. When no sound except raucous laughter was heard, he directed a boatswain, "Get yourself over to the Charleston Hotel and let the governor know he has one less nuisance on his hands."

Turned over to South Carolina authorities by her crew, the *Aiken* remained idle only one month. Empty, the vessel weighed almost eighty-three tons, making it just large enough to play havoc with the blockade recently proclaimed by Abraham Lincoln. Her two six-pounders, designed to halt smugglers, were small, but they were swivel-mounted for ease in use.

Ten residents of Charleston, headed by William Whaley, formed a limited partnership and purchased the cutter from the state. William Perry accepted an offer to take command in return for 10 percent of the prize money. Finding it more difficult to sign on a full crew of thirty-eight than he had expected, he could not sail until late July.

Meanwhile, the owners had secured from Richmond—the new seat of the Confederate government—the necessary letters of marque and reprisal. Thus the schooner, whose name had been changed to the *Petrel,* was operating under the auspices of the Confederate government when she sailed just after daylight on Sunday, July 28.

To the surprise and delight of Perry and his men, their first potential prize was sighted before the raider had been out of the harbor an hour. Bearing north-northeast, the unknown vessel appeared to be hugging the shore while following a heavily traveled sea lane leading to Philadelphia, New York, and Boston.

As the privateer closed on her target, still obscured by swirling fog, the anxious sailors ran up the Confederate colors. "Give her both guns, across her stern!" Perry ordered, envisioning his share of the cigars, rum, and sugar seized on the very first day's run. The little guns fired within seconds of each other.

Peering eagerly toward the strange vessel, Perry waited expectantly for it to heave to. Instead, to his horror he saw flames belch from what appeared to be a forecastle battery an instant before he heard the ear-rattling report of large naval cannon. No merchantman, the ship he had tried to stop was the USS *St. Lawrence,* a member of the blockading North Atlantic Squadron that had reached Charleston waters on July 27.

Trained gunners aboard the Federal warship hit their target squarely with their first salvo. By the time the startled Confederates realized what had happened, the *Petrel* was sinking rapidly. Two men went down with her, but the remaining thirty-six were pulled out of the water by the Federal crew.

When word of the one-sided naval engagement reached the U.S. secretary of the navy, Gideon Welles, in Washington, he ordered the prisoners to be transferred to the USS *Flag* at Savannah. Sailing from the Georgia port on August 3, the Federal cutter delivered them to Philadelphia five days later.

Meanwhile, Welles had contacted the flag officer of the Atlantic Squadron. Silas H. Stringham dutifully reported on August 12 that he had taken responsibility for securing witnesses from the crew of the *St. Lawrence* to testify in court and "condemn the pirates taken from the *Petrel.*" Soon C. S. Cotton and Ezekiel Buckmaster arrived in Hampton Roads to serve as witnesses for the United States against the pirates of the Confederate raider.

Federal records indicate that marshal James Millward of Philadelphia took nine of the thirty-six prisoners into his personal custody. Under orders of the U.S. secretary of state, William H. Seward, seven of these were transferred to Fort Lafayette in February: Richard Lewis, Austin C. Williams, Hugh Monagrow, Robert Barret, Thomas Brookbanks, John Dearing, and A. C. Delhay. The eighth man, Frank Albor, never left Philadelphia, having died in prison on November 9.

The remaining men from the *Petrel* who faced execution for the crime of piracy seem to have gone to other prisons. It is thought that

Perry and those of his men who survived the rigors of prison life were eventually exchanged.

The Charlestonians who had invested in the *Petrel* took the failure of their scheme philosophically. When the ten men came together to dissolve their limited partnership, Thomas J. Legare reputedly offered a few words of wisdom: "We lost, gentlemen. But each of us—and the entire South—can take pride in the fact that our gallant Confederates fired the first two shots in the first ship-to-ship engagement of the war."

It was a token distinction. Perry's pair of 6-pounders had challenged a vessel with ten 8-inch naval cannon, forty 32-pounders, and one heavy and one light 12-pounder. Thus when he launched the first ship-to-ship battle of the war, the ratio by which the "gallant" 83-ton *Petrel* was outgunned by the 1,708-ton *St. Lawrence* was approximately 109:1!

27

Abraham Lincoln

Maryland! MY Maryland!

ROBERT M. DENISON OF Baltimore County, Maryland, addressed his protest to the U.S. secretary of state, William H. Seward, from prison on December 28, 1861:

> In my arrest none of the forms of law heretofore existing in Maryland have been complied with; the arrest, however, was none the less potent and my imprisonment is none the less secure. It is plain so far as Maryland is concerned there has been a revolution in government; that the power of her courts and the protection which they afforded to her citizens have been usurped by the Government at Washington. We are taught that the Department thereof of which you are the head determines who shall be arrested in Maryland, how arrested, where imprisoned, and when released.

Denison and other members of the Maryland legislature had been arrested during a ten-day period in mid-September. First imprisoned in Baltimore's Fort McHenry, they were then sent to Fort Warren at Boston and placed in guarded casemates holding ten to twelve men. This wholesale incarceration of elected state officials constituted the second act of a drama that had begun sixty days earlier.

HARPER'S ILLUSTRATED HISTORY OF THE GREAT REBELLION

Federal military might led to raising the Stars and Stripes over the customs house at Baltimore.

Baltimore civilians engaged in a deadly contest with soldiers of the Sixth Massachusetts Militia on April 19. Bridges were burned and the city went wild in a demonstration of hostility toward the Federal government. Thus troops headed for Washington City had to be rerouted in a long detour that created fear and frustration in the Federal capital.

Baltimore-born journalist and songwriter James R. Randall responded to the riot by writing "Maryland, My Maryland." The lyrics were designed to embolden Secessionists in the city, and the song became universally popular in the South.

It did not take a military expert to see that if Maryland should follow Virginia's lead and withdraw from the Union, the central government would be in dire peril. To alarmists it seemed that there were enough vocal Secessionists in the state to make this possible or even probable.

LOSSING'S PICTORIAL FIELD BOOK OF THE CIVIL WAR

Baltimore's police chief, George P. Kane, made no secret of his sympathy for Secessionists.

Abraham Lincoln agonized over the unexpected crisis, then decided upon drastic action to ensure that Maryland would not secede. Since George P. Kane was the police chief when the riot happened, an example would have to be made of him. Never mind that he had submitted a lengthy report to the board of police on May 3, describing his actions on the fateful afternoon. Forget that Kane had consulted both the mayor and the governor, both of whom felt that the bridges had to be burned to prevent the collision certain to result from the passage of more troops through the divided state. Strike out or ignore one paragraph in Kane's report in which he wrote that Baltimore "seemed filled with horror at the knowledge that peaceful and respected citizens had been shot on our public streets [by volunteers responding to Lincoln's call]."

Kane would have to go. Since there was no reason to believe he would do so voluntarily, he would have to be arrested and confined. Also, the commissioners to whom he reported and who approved his actions would have to go with him. Acting on behalf of the president, the secretary of state, William H. Seward, directed Brig. Gen. Nathaniel P. Banks, commander of a division within the Department of Annapolis, to make the necessary arrests.

Kane was roused from his bed at 3:00 A.M. on June 27 and taken to Fort McHenry for confinement. On July 1 nine companies of men from the Sixth Massachusetts arrested the police commissioner, Charles Howard. Simultaneously, four companies of the Eighteenth

Pennsylvania seized commissioner William H. Gatchell. A single detachment—seven companies of the Twenty-second Pennsylvania—took commissioners John W. Davis and Charles D. Hinks into custody.

All official orders referred to these men as no longer holding office, although none had resigned and no election had been held. Col. John R. Kenly of the First Maryland, selected by Banks to function as provost marshal of Baltimore, immediately organized a force of four hundred men to serve as police officers. Brig. Gen. John A. Dix, who was in command on September 3, ordered Baltimore Mayor George W. Brown to see that all payments to the old city police were stopped.

With the riot-torn city firmly under military control and officials who might cause trouble under arrest, everything should have returned to normal, but it did not. Several members of the legislature had Southern sympathies or were suspected of having such sentiments. The lawmakers were scheduled to hold a special session at Frederick City, beginning on September 16. If they should vote for secession when they came together, the president threatened more arrests.

Fuel was added to the fire when Seward received a letter from W. G. Snethen of Baltimore. According to him, the rebellion had suffered "a staggering blow" by the "arrest of the traitors," but he was wary that if the legislature convened the state might still secede. "There are thin-skinned Union men enough who will seek to get a quorum for the sake of the $4 a day [they receive as pay]," he warned.

Seward needed little if any prodding; he agreed with Lincoln that the loss of Maryland could tip the scales toward a Southern victory. Maj. Gen. George B. McClellan, who thought highly of detective Allan Pinkerton, sent him into Maryland. Consultation with General Dix led Pinkerton to conclude that Mayor Brown of Baltimore was as dangerous as were members of the legislature whose arrest had been authorized in Washington.

With the support of the military police, on September 12 Pinkerton oversaw a midnight sweep of Baltimore. Early on the following morning his detectives committed the mayor and eight legislators to Fort McHenry.

The men now behind bars were considered the core Secessionists capable of leading Maryland out of the Union. Many lawmakers residing outside the city were outraged at the arrest of their colleagues; hence they were seen as possibly sharing their political views. That meant the original scheme for holding Maryland in the Union had to be enlarged. The arrests continued throughout the fall, and the Maryland legislature did not hold its scheduled special session.

Offered an opportunity to take an oath of allegiance to the United States, a few legislators behind bars accepted to gain their freedom. By far the most colorful and influential of those who gained an early release was Ross G. Winans, a wealthy industrialist.

In rapid success, Brig. Gens. Benjamin F. Butler and George Cadwalader succeeded to command of the District of Annapolis. One of Cadwalader's adjutants, E. D. Townsend, learned on May 16 that his chief had "just been instructed by the highest authority" to offer freedom to Winans. Only one condition was stipulated: he must give his parole of honor not to commit any act of hostility against the United States.

Undocumented lore has it that Lincoln had his eye on a device put together by some of Winans's employees. At his instruction, they fashioned a piece of steam-powered artillery that was mounted on a railroad car. Tradition has it that the president felt this weapon to be potentially decisive; as a result, he is said to have facilitated Winans's freedom.

Cadwalader, who did not know that Winans was being held as a prisoner at Fort McHenry until informed by Townsend, promptly sent an officer to inform the legislator of terms offered to him. "The result," wrote Cadwalader, "was that Mr. Winans signed the parole and was immediately liberated."

On May 18, Butler dashed off a furious dispatch to the secretary of war, saying in part:

> I have just received an order from General Scott transferring the command of the Department of Annapolis to General Cadwalader and ordering me to Fort Monroe [to take command there]. What does this mean? Is it a censure upon my action? Is it because I have caused Winans to be arrested? Cadwalader may release Winans—probably will. You must guard against that. To be relieved of a command of a department and sent to command a fort, without a word of comment, is something unusual at least. [Hence] I desire a personal interview with you and with the President before I accept further service.

Exactly one month after Butler voiced his surprise and dissatisfaction, he had a brief meeting with Lincoln, but no record of the conversation survives.

Numerous prominent Marylanders remained in custody for weeks and months. Brown's case was pled late in November in a letter to F. W. Seward, assistant secretary of state. According to Baltimore citizen S. C. Hawley, on April 19—the day of the riot—"Brown marched with the troops at the peril of his life and heroically did all in his power to give them safe conduct."

Early and angry reactions to the wholesale arrests were not limited to the people of Maryland. On July 24 the U.S. House of Representatives adopted a resolution asking the president to explain his actions. Lincoln replied promptly and briefly on July 27: "It is . . . incompatible with the public interest at this time to furnish the information called for by the resolution."

Another resolution was submitted in the Senate calling for the commissioners and the chief of police to be surrendered to civil authorities or released to resume their duties. In the House of Representatives, a resolution was introduced declaring the Baltimore arrests "flagrantly unconstitutional and illegal." Galusha A. Grow of Pennsylvania, Speaker of the House, acted swiftly and declared the resolution inadmissible.

In early August Seward received word that Baltimore's former police commissioners had "taken measures to sue out a writ of habeas corpus." He therefore asked Gen. Winfield Scott to send a telegram instructing the officer in command not to obey the writ. Scott, who had dispatched precisely such instructions on August 2, repeated them on August 8.

A Brooklyn judge had already issued a writ commanding Lt. Col. Martin Burke, commandant of the fort, to produce the prisoners before the King's County Court. When Burke refused, a warrant for his arrest was issued, but the sheriff was prevented from serving it. Inquiry by the judge revealed that members of the New York militia were "quite destitute of artillery" and hence were unable to help enforce the orders of the court. As a result a formal ruling was issued stating that "the power of the Court was exhausted," and there was no other formal attempt to free the prisoners from Maryland.

On October 8, Brown, Kane and seventy-four other prisoners addressed a protest to Lincoln concerning conditions at Fort Lafayette. Matters, they said, "could hardly be worse if they were in a slave ship on the middle passage." Numerous prisoners were in irons; some had no beds, bedding "or any of the commonest necessities."

This appeal led to a perfunctory inspection of four small casemates and two large battery rooms in which the political prisoners were held. Conditions, reported Burke, were as good as possible under unusual circumstances.

Dates and conditions under which Maryland officials gained their release seldom appear in surviving records. Some were home by the time of the harvest season, but many others remained at Fort

Lafayette. On December 4 Brown was given a thirty-day release "on his parole not to leave the New England States nor to do any act hostile or injurious to the United States." He accepted that release, then surrendered himself on January 4, 1862.

Recommitted to Fort Warren, the elected mayor of Baltimore remained angry that his functions were being discharged by an appointee of the provost marshal. Brown was still in custody on February 15, when all political prisoners were transferred from custody of the State Department to the War Department.

The *Official Records* later noted, "There are no papers in the State Department concerning the precise character of the charges against Brown." Among the last to be released, along with police chief Kane, he remained behind bars until November 1862.

To prevent civil authorities from defeating his scheme concerning Maryland, the president took unprecedented action on April 26. Through Scott he notified Butler—then in command at Baltimore—that he was authorized "to adopt the most prompt and efficient means" to deal with Secessionists. If necessary, Butler must order "the bombardment of their cities, and in the extremest necessity suspension of the writ of habeas corpus."

Suspension of the time-honored legal order "to produce the body" of a person under arrest effectively foiled plans of persons seeking to gain the release of Marylanders. Repeated several times and eventually extended to the entire Union, the suspension is still high on the list of Lincoln's most controversial actions that he termed the "exercise of war powers."

The president's April call for seventy-five thousand volunteers evoked astonishment and rage in many regions. Maryland's reaction probably would have been no more memorable than that in numerous other states had not a soldier-civilian clash in Baltimore produced the first significant number of deaths in the mounting confrontation.

Clearly, the port city close to the Federal capital included numerous residents of pro-Southern sentiment who were loud and persistent in making their views known. No one knows what would have happened had Lincoln not implemented a scheme to foil those leaders who were eager to take Maryland out of the Union. Although the president's actions led the Union dangerously close to becoming a police state ruled by the military, arrests of lawmakers and other officials and private citizens served their purpose. Maryland did not secede, so only a fraction of her money and manpower went to the South.

28

Two Virginias

The Mountaineers and the Gentry

With the danger of sectional strife mounting rapidly, many Virginians wanted nothing so much as compromise. On January 19, 1861, this yearning led the Old Dominion to invite every state to participate in a peace convention. It convened in Washington on February 4, the day delegates from the already seceded states assembled in Montgomery, Alabama, to establish the Confederate States of America.

Former president John Tyler presided over the Washington Peace Conference that eventually included 131 representatives from 21 states. Despite a zeal for peace on the part of many who participated, there was, unfortunately, not enough spirit of compromise, so the convention dissolved without having a significant impact.

Even after the failure of the peace conference, many Virginians with strong ties to the seceded states were far from ready to join them. Unionist sentiment was strong when a secession convention began meeting in Richmond. In no other state did this divisiveness have more important political repercussions.

Yet public opposition to secession faded the second week in April when Abraham Lincoln responded to the surrender of Fort Sumter by calling for seventy-five thousand volunteers. Many who wavered felt

Former president John Tyler sided with the Confederacy and was ostracized in Washington.

a primary loyalty to Virginia. On April 19, two days after Lincoln's proclamation, eighty-eight Secessionist delegates to the Richmond convention overwhelmed fifty-five Unionist colleagues. The delegates from the mountainous western regions of the state were especially divided in their loyalties. Some changed their minds after having cast their votes; eventually twenty-eight of them remained opposed to secession, while fifteen supported it.

Once secession was approved, the Unionists of western Virginia began planning their own strategy. The precedent just established seemed to justify similar action. A delegate offered this response to the Southern revolt against the national government:

> The right of revolution can be exercised as well by a portion of the citizens of a State against their State government, as it can be exercised by the whole people of a State against their Federal Government. Any change of the relation Virginia now sustains to the Federal Government, made against the wishes of even a respectable minority of her people would justify them in changing their relation to the State Government by separating themselves from that section of the State that had thus wantonly disregarded their interests and defied their will.

THEODORE R. DAVIS SKETCH

Small farmers of western Virginia seldom if ever attended slave auctions—slaves were valueless in the mountains.

Few citizens west of the Alleghenies owned slaves and had little in common with the powerful landed gentry in the east. The region's major rivers and roads ran north and south, and western Virginian culture and economy were more similar to Pennsylvania and Ohio than Richmond and Norfolk. Wheeling, the largest city of the region, was more than three hundred miles from Richmond but only sixty miles from Pittsburgh.

Manor houses surrounded by huge plantations were abundant in the east, while cabins of lumbermen and miners abounded in the west. Taxes collected by Richmond were used to support roads and other public improvements that lay almost exclusively on the Chesapeake Bay side of the mountains. An asylum planned at Weston, but not yet built, represented the largest expenditure of public funds in thirty-five counties west of the Shenandoah Valley and north of the Kanawah River. Except in the valley of the Kanawah and along the line of the Baltimore and Ohio Railroad, the west was marked by occasional rural settlements and villages rather than by clusters of towns and cities.

The degree of domination exercised by eastern Virginians became evident in 1851 when special legislation was passed regarding slaves. Under its terms, the maximum taxable value of a slave became three hundred dollars, and those under age twelve were excluded from taxation. About one-fourth of the state's white population lay in the west, but it included only eighteen thousand of Virginia's half-million slaves.

On May 23, 1861, Virginia's secession ordinance was submitted to popular vote. When the ballots were tallied, 125,950 voters supported secession and 10,373 opposed, with returns from thirty-four counties in the west not having been received.

On June 11 a body of delegates—some probably self-appointed—came to Wheeling to "cut ties with [the] conspirators at Richmond." Led by Ohio-born Archibald W. Campbell of the *Wheeling Intelligencer,* the rump body disavowed all allegiance to the Confederacy. Two months later, delegates from twenty-six counties created the new state of Kanawah, consisting of forty-eight counties (two were added later), with its capital at Wheeling.

The "Restored Government of Virginia" chose Francis H. Pierpont to serve as governor and John S. Carlile and Waitman T. Willy as senators. By November a state constitution for West Virginia had been drafted; it was ratified April 3, 1862, by voters who swore allegiance to the United States. On May 13, 1862, the new state legislature then petitioned the U.S. Congress to admit the thirty-fifth state into the Union.

In Washington, the attorney general, Edward Bates, was opposed to this action. To his diary he confided that the Wheeling government was made up of "a few reckless Radicals, who manage those helpless puppets as a gamester manages his marked cards." The secretary of the navy, Gideon Welles, and the postmaster general, Montgomery Blair, also believed that the admission of West Virginia rested on unconstitutional actions.

Article 4 section 3 of the U.S. Constitution specified: "No new State shall be formed or erected within the jurisdiction of any other State, nor any State formed by the junction of two or more States or parts of States, without the consent of the Legislatures of the States concerned, as well as of the Congress."

Congress, nevertheless, voted approval. Although Lincoln considered vetoing the bill, he reluctantly signed it. Statehood was granted with the proviso that slavery would be abolished. On June 20, 1863, West Virginia formally joined the Union, and Republican Arthur I. Boreman was elected the first governor.

These political maneuvers were facilitated by a string of Union military victories in the region: Philippi, Laurel Hill, Rich Mountain, and Corrick's Ford. The Federal commander who engineered this campaign and established permanent control over this portion of the state was George B. McClellan. At the same time, Confederate forces were uncoordinated and thinly manned. Even the presence of Robert E. Lee, dispatched from Richmond on special duty, was not enough to bolster the Southern military presence in western Virginia.

By the time the political question of statehood became paramount, a thinly veiled Federal solution had been devised. Virginia now had governments in three capitals: Richmond, Wheeling, and Alexandria. Respectively, they represented: Secessionists, advocates for western independence, and the restored government of Virginia.

Since Wheeling could hardly provide the consent to its own recognition, Washington turned to the Unionist government in exile in Alexandria, which was occupied by Federal troops. Officials of that unrecognized government, representing less than 5 percent of the state, solemnly sanctioned the division of the Old Dominion and the creation of West Virginia. Hence it was by means of one of the most devious exploits of the Lincoln administration that the thirty-fifth state—without the traditional probationary period when the area would be treated as a territory—was admitted to the Union, emerging as a full-blown state and guaranteeing the president its electoral votes in 1864.

It may be said that the Civil War created West Virginia, but the fledgling state endured its own civil war during those four years. Regular troops, partisans, and feuding clans generated a constant, bitter warfare across the region, similar to what was happening in Missouri. Yet during that time about twenty-five thousand West Virginians fought for the Union and fifteen thousand for the Confederacy. The wounds of war, however, required decades to heal.

29

Ulric Dahlgren

The Plot to Kill a President

ON APRIL 1, 1864, Confederate Gen. Robert E. Lee addressed an inquiry to Union Maj. Gen. George G. Meade, commander of the Army of the Potomac. Lee may have found it difficult to employ the polite language that was conventional between two enemy generals, for he had never before dealt with so explosive a matter.

His letter was accompanied by photographic copies of two documents found on the body of Union Col. Ulric Dahlgren near Richmond a few weeks earlier. One, he pointed out, bore "the official signature of Colonel Dahlgren, and the other, not signed, contained more detailed explanation of the purpose of [Dahlgren's] raid directed against Richmond."

At this point, the Confederate commander quoted a paragraph from one of the documents, a rough draft of an address to his men that also bore Dahlgren's signature: "We hope to release the prisoners from Belle Island first, and have seen them fairly started [toward the Union lines], we will cross the James River into Richmond, destroying the bridges after us and exhorting the released prisoners to destroy and burn the hateful city; and do not allow the rebel leader Davis and his traitorous crew to escape."

THE SOLDIER IN OUR CIVIL WAR

Although less important than the goal of kidnapping or killing Confederate leaders, Richmond's Libby Prison was a target of the Dahlgren raid.

The second document, Dahlgren's unsigned instructions, gave a brief but specific explanation of the mission's goal. Lee quoted two sentences: "The bridges once secured, and the prisoners loose and over the river, the bridges will be secured and the city destroyed. The men must keep together and well in hand, and once in the city it must be destroyed and Jeff. Davis and cabinet killed."

Having shared with Meade these damning words, Lee came to the purpose of his writing: "I beg leave respectfully to inquire whether the designs and instructions of Colonel Dahlgren, as set for this these papers, were authorized by the United States Government or by his superior officers, and also whether they have the sanction and approval of these authorities."

Meade and every other high-ranking Federal officer and official who became involved denied that the action had been authorized. They claimed that the papers were forgeries.

To support their assessment of the papers, they called on Dahlgren's father, Rear Adm. John A. Dahlgren. The admiral had invented three types of cannon during the decade before the war,

Adm. John A. Dahlgren was positive that papers found on the body of his son had been forged by Confederates.

when he directed the U.S. Navy's ordnance department: bronze boat howitzers and rifles, iron smoothbore shellguns, and iron rifles. At the outbreak of the war he was in command of the Washington Naval Yard and in July 1862 was made chief of the Bureau of Ordnance. Dahlgren applied for sea duty and was posted to command the South Atlantic Blockading Squadron. For most of the war he was involved with operations against Charleston.

When the elder Dahlgren was shown the photographs of the Dahlgren papers, he examined the all-important signature to the first document and immediately denounced it. "This is not my son's signature," he insisted. "That being the case, these documents are clumsy forgeries. Their only purpose is to blacken the name of my son, his men, and those who gave him orders." Controversy over the authenticity of one of the most inflammatory sets of papers that surfaced during the Civil War continued for more than a century after their bearer died with them in his pocket.

Praised as "exceptional" and "able and ambitious" by his commanding officers, Ulric had gained a commission through his father's influence. An 1862 letter from Abraham Lincoln to U.S. Secretary of War Edwin M. Stanton made young Dahlgren a lieutenant, not in the United States Volunteers, but in the U.S. Army. He was attached to

The Dahlgren gun was widely used on Federal warships and was one of the most formidable-looking weapons of the war.

Franz Siegel's Eleventh Corps and served as an artillery commander at Second Manassas.

In the year that followed, Dahlgren served as an aide to Ambrose Burnside at Fredericksburg, to Joseph Hooker at Chancellorsville, and to Meade at Gettysburg. In May 1863 he captured a courier carrying dispatches to Lee explaining that reinforcements would not available for his invasion of the North, and that information strongly influenced Meade to hold Lee at Gettysburg rather than fall back into Maryland. During the Confederate retreat from Pennsylvania, Dahlgren joined a cavalry division under Gen. Judson Kilpatrick that tried to block the withdrawal. In street fighting in Hagerstown, Maryland, Dahlgren was severely wounded and lost a leg. While recuperating and rehabilitating with an artificial limb, he may have developed the plot that later made him infamous in the South.

Meanwhile, on December 8, 1863, President Lincoln delivered his annual message to Congress in which he said, "The crisis which threatened to divide the friends of the Union is Past." Thus, said Lincoln, it was time to make plans to bring the wayward states back into

H. W. SMITH ENGRAVING

Judson Kilpatrick— or some other general—almost certainly received clearance for the Richmond raid from the president or one of his top aides.

the family of the Union. He proposed a proclamation of amnesty and reconstruction. It offered a full pardon to all Confederates except certain classes. To qualify for that pardon, one must take an oath to protect and defend the Constitution of the United States, and the union of the states, and promise to abide by a few other stipulations.

The president hoped his amnesty plan would restore peace and harmony to the divided nation. Once the proclamation was printed, arrangements were made to try to get copies into Southern territory. By late January, the president realized that his amnesty plan was producing few results. Perhaps his proclamation was not reaching the proper persons, he concluded.

It took a month for Kilpatrick to devise a plan to free Federal prisoners in Richmond through a raid during which copies of the amnesty proclamation could be distributed. He was authorized to proceed with about five thousand men without detailed instructions.

By late February Kilpatrick's command included Dahlgren, who "with some 600 picked men went an hour in advance of the main column" that was headed toward the Confederate capital. Capt. Joseph Gloskoski, a signal officer of the Twenty-ninth New York Infantry, later reported that on the night of February 28 at Spotsylvania Court House, Dahlgren and his men parted from the principal body of raiders.

Kilpatrick's troops encountered a winter storm so severe, reported Gloskoski, that "sharp wind and sleet forced men to close their eyes." Although they had taken separate paths, both groups of Federal soldiers headed toward Richmond in the darkness. Soon a signal officer sent up several rockets but received no response from Dahlgren's men.

The main strike force reached Richmond about noon on March 1. Instead of meeting token resistance, they were met by a storm of bullets. After fighting until nightfall, the raiders abandoned their efforts and withdrew northward toward the Pamunkey River. On the following day, some four hundred or more of Dahlgren's detachment rejoined Kilpatrick's force, but their colonel was not with them.

Survivors differed only in some details of the story they reported. Failing to cross the James River as planned, Dahlgren had moved toward Richmond with about eighty men and two ambulances. It proved impossible to liberate the prisoners as planned, and the party turned back toward the Federal lines. While headed toward Gloucester Court House

A small boy's role in the Dahlgren saga was not unusual; an estimated sixty thousand served in uniform as drummers.

in King and Queen County, they ran into an ambush in which Dahlgren and several others were killed and most of the rest were captured.

The Confederate secretary of war, James A. Seddon, described the soldiers who scored this minor victory as a body of "local reserves, composed of clerks, recently organized, and untried in war." Their commander was Edward W. Halback, a teacher. One member of his militia company was thirteen-year-old William Littlepage, who was greedy or curious or both. It was the boy who searched the body of Dahlgren and found the papers in the officer's pockets, which he turned over to Halback.

Dispatched to Richmond with word that the documents might be of importance, the Dahlgren papers were examined with care and pronounced genuine. Soon Southern newspapers reprinted both documents in full, accompanied by scathing editorials that denounced the savage and demonic minds of the Federal planners. It took much longer to make the photographic copies that Lee transmitted to Meade along with his polite demand for an explanation.

Federal protestations about forgeries, coupled with angry Confederate accusations, echoed for months. A few of those who handled the original documents pointed out that they were uncommonly difficult to read. The writer had used thin paper and some of his ink had seeped through and obscured the writing on the other side of the paper. This aspect of the pen-written documents was particularly noticeable in the signature.

More than a decade after the Southern surrender at Appomattox, former Confederate Gen. Jubal Early was permitted to look at the captured documents. He noticed that some of the letters and a few words that had oozed through the paper could be deciphered with a mirror. Ink that had bled from one side of a page to the other, said Early, could account for the apparently garbled signature. Hence he leaned toward the belief that the Dahlgren papers were genuine.

Early's verdict was supported by a record of the interrogation of Capt. John McEntee, who was with Dahlgren when he died. McEntee believed that the papers were genuine because their words were similar to what Dahlgren had said to him.

As time passed and tempers cooled on both sides, the controversial papers were shifted in storage from place to place until records concerning their location were lost. After several decades, they were rediscovered and examined by experts who could find no evidence of forgery or tampering.

Today it is conceded that in March 1864 there was a plot to burn Richmond and kill the Confederate president and members of his cabinet. That conclusion fails, however, to establish the identity of the person who authorized Dahlgren to proceed with his plan. Military leaders have always generally agreed that he could not have led the raid without approval. If that judgment is correct, someone high in the Lincoln administration must have given Dahlgren permission to act. At the same time, Meade harbored suspicions that Kilpatrick was behind the scheme and privately alluded to what he called "collateral evidence" that cast doubt on the cavalry commander's version of the mission planning. Now, after so much time has elapsed, it is unlikely that the identity of the person who approved Dahlgren's plot will ever be found.

30

John Wilkes Booth

The Last Plot

In 1859 news that abolitionist John Brown had captured the U.S. arsenal at Harpers Ferry, Virginia, threw the state into turmoil. Militia, called out to subdue Brown and his followers, accepted into their ranks anyone willing to fight. That is how a Maryland civilian "had the honor of fighting for the South at the Ferry." The next day marines from the Washington Naval Yard arrived under the command of Lt. Col. Robert E. Lee and his adjutant, Lt. James Ewell Brown "Jeb" Stuart.

Only twenty-one years old, John Wilkes Booth of Harford County, Maryland, was keenly aware of the divided sentiment in his native state. Although outspokenly zealous for the southern cause, his only military activity in its behalf was his peripheral involvement in the 1859 capture of Brown. Nothing enraged him more, however, than the swift arrest of prominent Secessionists in Maryland in 1861, which kept the state in the Union.

Booth alternated between bragging about his exploits, brooding over the future, and blaming Abraham Lincoln for the misfortunes of the South. When he heard that the fall of Atlanta virtually guaranteed the president's reelection, he fell into a deep depression.

Continuing Confederate misfortunes inflated the number of men held in Union prison camps to new heights. Pondering the conditions under which many of these men lived—little better than Yankee prisoners at Andersonville in Georgia—Booth had an inspiration. A small band of bold men, he reasoned, could kidnap the president of the United States. His freedom would be offered in return for the release of many or most Confederate prisoners.

Late in 1864 the aspiring actor found men he considered trustworthy and who shared his passion for the South. They included Sam Arnold and Michael O'Laughlin—both of whom he had known for most of his life, George Atzerodt—who had helped escaping Confederates to reach Virginia, and John Surratt—who had boasted that he played a major role in the Confederate Secret Service.

These men, along with others who were judged to be less trustworthy, met with some frequency at a Washington boarding house operated by Mary Surratt. Late in 1864 they perfected their plan to kidnap the president. When he attended a theatrical performance in mid-January, with relays of horses stationed along a predetermined route, the bound and gagged president could be headed for Richmond before any Federal officials realized what had happened.

The plan was not bad. One conspirator was sent to Maryland to obtain horses. Atzerodt investigated the lease of a flatboat, since the regular ferry might be watched. Surratt learned the layout of Ford's Theater, particularly the large valve that controlled the gaslights. With the theater darkened, Lincoln could be rushed into a wagon before anyone knew what was happening. The only problem was that Lincoln was not in the audience on the night Booth had set for the kidnapping. Discouraged but not dissuaded, Booth recruited another conspirator, Lewis Paine, a former Confederate soldier.

Booth learned that Lincoln and his wife planned to attend a theatrical performance at Campbell Hospital in February 1865. The Lincoln carriage would have to use the only road that led directly to the hospital from the heart of the capital. Hence five of the conspirators hid at a point along the route and prepared to abduct the president. For a second time Booth and his recruits were foiled. Lincoln had canceled his plan to see the performance at the hospital.

There is little documentary evidence concerning Booth's third plot. At Lincoln's second inauguration on March 4, 1865, photographer Alexander Gardner made a number of exposures. Not until a century had passed did anyone realize that Booth and five conspirators were only a few feet away from the president as he delivered his

LIBRARY OF CONGRESS

Ford's Theater was the setting for one of the most tragic moments in American history.

second inaugural address. All six of them can be seen and identified in enhanced prints of one of Gardner's photographs.

It is possible that by the time of the inauguration, kidnapping may have been abandoned in favor of assassination. Whether or not that was the case, tight security may have convinced Booth that any action that day would be futile.

Thereafter events moved swiftly. In late March the president paid an extended visit to U. S. Grant's army at City Point, Virginia, where civilians had no chance to get close to the president. While at City Point, Lincoln received word of the fall of Richmond and quickly arranged to visit the former Confederate capital. There someone handed him a Confederate bill, and Lincoln placed it in his wallet as a souvenir. He did not return to Washington until April 9, when he received word of Robert E. Lee's surrender at Appomattox Court House.

Greatly relieved with the war largely over, Lincoln's routine for the next several days was quite calm. On Good Friday, his son, Robert, gave him a firsthand account of the events at the surrender, and the president had a series of lengthy meetings.

That morning he had told Capt. Thomas T. Eckert of his plans to attend Ford's Theater and invited him to come along as his guest. The president was going in response to a special invitation from John Ford and anticipated seeing Laura Keene in the title role of *Our American Cousin.* Eckert declined, as did General and Mrs. Grant and Secretary and Mrs. Stanton. Then the president invited Maj. Henry R. Rathbone, who accepted and brought along Clara Harris, his fiancée.

Booth learned of the president's possible attendance and decided to put his revised plot into motion. Having picked up his mail at the theater during the morning, he returned to cut a peephole that would give him a view of the presidential box.

Four conspirators are believed to have met about 8:00 P.M. to coordinate their efforts. Atzerodt was given the important assignment of killing Vice President Andrew Johnson. Since Secretary of State William H. Seward had recently been injured and was believed to have military attendants, two men were assigned to him. As for Lincoln, Booth chose to pull the trigger himself.

Frederick Seward, the secretary's son, and George T. Robinson of the Eighth Maine Regiment were keeping watch over the injured cabinet member on the evening of Good Friday. At around ten o'clock, Robinson heard someone on the stairway. When the younger Seward went to the door to check, he encountered "a giant of a man wearing well-worn clothing."

Paine tried to shoot Frederick, but his weapon did not fire. He then used the gun as a club and gave the secretary's son two deep gashes on his head. Discarding his revolver in favor of a knife, he slashed Robinson and Frederick's brother Augustus, who had been awakened by the commotion. Seward was not injured, but few men targeted by an enraged killer have had a more narrow escape from death.

Atzerodt, meanwhile, who was under orders to dispose of the vice president, lost his nerve and left the city. Booth, who wanted all assassinations to take place simultaneously, reached the theater about 8:30 and had plenty of time for a few drinks to boost his courage.

Booth reached the vicinity of the presidential box without challenge, and about 10:00 opened the door to slip inside it. With his derringer close to the president's head, he fired a single fatal shot before leaping from the box to the stage below. His spur caught in a flag, however, and when the actor hit the stage, his left leg was broken.

HARPER'S WEEKLY

The assassination of President Lincoln by John Wilkes Booth stunned the nation just as the people glimpsed the end of the Civil War. To many, Lincoln was considered the last casualty of the war. Had Booth's spur not caught in an ornamental flag, he might have escaped without injury, but his capture was inevitable as were those of his coconspirators.

As rapidly as pain would permit, Booth hobbled to a waiting horse and then talked a guard into permitting him to cross a bridge over the Potomac River. Detouring from his planned route, he managed to persuade a retired physician, Samuel Mudd, to set his broken leg. Meanwhile, authorities in Washington launched a massive manhunt and published posters offering huge rewards.

Twelve days later, Booth was trapped in a tobacco barn near Port Royal, Virginia. Soldiers led by Lt. Edward P. Doherty surrounded it and ordered its occupants to surrender. David Herold meekly obeyed and was handcuffed and roped to a nearby tree. When Booth ignored the commands, the barn was set on fire to drive him out. As the flames spread, Sgt. Boston Corbett shot and mortally wounded its solitary occupant.

Before Booth was apprehended, numerous persons associated with the conspirators had been arrested on suspicion of having aided them. John T. Ford, principal owner of the theater that bore his name, languished in Old Capitol Prison for more than a month; two of his brothers were also locked up. Units of soldiers who were under orders from the secretary of war rounded up every known Confederate sympathizer in the capital and incarcerated most of them.

Attorney General James Speed, an old acquaintance of the martyred president, advised the new president, Andrew Johnson, to establish a special military tribunal. Headed by Maj. Gen. David Hunter, the nine-man commission convened on May 9 and acted swiftly and harshly.

Late in June, persons considered to have played significant roles in Booth's plots were sentenced to death. Among them was boardinghouse keeper Mary Surratt. Sentenced to life imprisonment, Dr. Samuel Mudd's name was cleared generations later through the tireless work of his descendants.

Three men and one woman, judged in 1865 to have been most closely involved with Booth, were hanged on July 7. That day they paid with their lives for having been acquainted with the first man successfully to plan the assassination of an American president.

LIBRARY OF CONGRESS

Booth died shortly after his apprehension. Mary Surratt, Lewis Paine, George Atzerodt, and David Herold were hanged simultaneously on July 7, 1865, in the Washington Naval Yard. Secretary of State Edwin M. Stanton said afterward, "Let their names no longer be heard."

Theories of a wider conspiracy have persisted despite flimsy evidence. Numerous high-ranking civil and military leaders, including Secretary of War Stanton, have been suggested as implicated in the plot. Most historians dismiss them.

After the assassination, Southerners brought forward their own sets of arguments. They pointed out that Booth was never a Confederate soldier, nor a resident of the Confederacy. Thus, they argued, he acted out of anger at the actions of the Federal authorities. Writing of Lincoln in his intimate journal, Booth noted, "Our country owed all her troubles to him, and God simply made me the instrument of His punishment."

BIBLIOGRAPHY

Abott, Henry Livermore. *Fallen Leaves.* Kent, Ohio: Kent State University Press, 1991.
American Heritage, 1961.
American History Illustrated, 1976.
Baird, Nancy D. "The Yellow Fever Plot." *Civil War Times Illustrated,* November 1974.
Basler, Roy P. *The Collected Works of Abraham Lincoln.* New Brunswick: Rutgers University Press, 1953.
Bastian, David F. *Grant's Canal.* Shippensburg, Pa.: Burd Street, 1995.
Bogle, James G. "The Great Locomotive Chase." *Blue & Gray* (June-July 1987).
Bowers, John. *Stonewall Jackson.* New York: Morrow, 1988.
Buell, Clarence C., and Robert U. Johnson, eds. *Battles and Leaders of the Civil War.* 4 vols. New York: Century, 1884–88. Reprint, Secaucus, N.J.: Castle, 1985.
Bushong, Millard K. *Old Jube.* Boyce, Va.: Carr, 1955.
Catton, Bruce. *American Heritage Picture History of the Civil War.* New York: Wings, 1982.
———. *The Army of the Potomac.* 3 vols. Garden City, N.Y.: Doubleday, 1951–53.
———. *Centennial History of the Civil War.* Garden City, N.Y.: Doubleday, 1961.
———. *The Civil War (Mr. Lincoln's Army, Glory Road, A Stillness at Appomattox).* New York: Fairfax, 1980.
———. *Glory Road.* Garden City, N.Y.: Doubleday, 1952.
———. *Grant Moves South.* Boston: Little, Brown, 1960.
———. *Mr. Lincoln's Army.* Garden City, N.Y.: Doubleday, 1961.
Chamberlain, Joshua L. *The Passing of the Armies.* New York: Putnam's, 1915.
Charleston Daily Courier. 1861–64.
Charleston Mercury. 1861–62.
Charleston Museum Archives.
Confederate Veteran. 1903–1932.
Coppee, Henry, ed. *History of the Civil War in America by the Comte de Paris.* 2 vols. Philadelphia: Coates, 1875.
Cornish, Dudley T. *The Sable Arm.* New York: Longmans, 1956.
Dahlgren, John A. *Memoir of Ulric Dahlgren.* Philadelphia: n.p., 1872.
Davis, Burke. *Jeb Stuart.* New York: Wings, 1957.
Davis, Varina. *Jefferson Davis.* New York: Bedford, 1890.
De Trobriand, Regis. *Four Years with the Army of the Potomac.* Boston: n.p., 1889.
DuBois, W. E. B. *John Brown.* New York: International, 1962.
Early, Jubal A. *Autobiographical Sketch.* Philadelphia: Lippincott, 1912.
———. *Narrative of the War Between the States.* Reprint, New York: Da Capo, 1992.
Eisencheml, Otto. *Why Was Lincoln Murdered?* Boston: Little, Brown, 1937.
———. *In the Shadow of Lincoln's Death.* New York: Funk, 1940.

———, and Ralph Newman. *The American Iliad.* Indianapolis: Bobbs-Merrill, 1947.
———. *Why the Civil War?* Indianapolis: Bobbs-Merrill, 1958.
Elliott, Charles W. *Winfield Scott: The Soldier and the Man.* New York: Macmillan, 1937.
Evans, Clement A., ed. *Confederate Military History.* 17 vols. Atlanta: Confederate, 1899.
Farwell, Byron. *Stonewall.* New York: Norton, 1992.
Faust, Patricial L., ed. *Historical Times Illustrated Encyclopedia of the Civil War.* New York: Harper & Row, 1986.
Frank Leslie's Illustrated History of the Civil War. New York, 1895.
Frank Leslie's Illustrated Weekly. 1861–65.
Gleeson, Ed. *Illinois Rebels.* Carmel, Ind.: Guild, 1997.
———. *Rebel Sons of Erin.* Indianapolis: Guild, 1993.
Grant, U. S. *Memoirs and Selected Letters.* 2 vols. New York: Literary Classics, 1990.
Gray, Wood. *The Hidden Civil War.* New York: Viking, 1942.
Greeley, Horace. *The American Conflict.* 2 vols. Hartford: O. D. Chase, 1866.
———. *The Tribune Almanac and Political Register for 1861.* New York: n.p., 1860.
———. *The Tribune Almanac and Political Register for 1862.* New York: n.p., 1861.
———. *The Tribune Almanac and Political Register for 1863.* New York: n.p., 1862.
———. *The Tribune Almanac and Political Register for 1864.* New York: n.p., 1863.
———. *The Tribune Almanac and Political Register for 1865.* New York: n.p., 1864.
Guerney, Gene. *A Pictorial History of the United States Army.* New York: Crown, 1972.
Hanchett, William. *The Lincoln Murder Conspiracies.* Urbana: University of Illinois Press, 1983.
Harper, Robert S. *Lincoln and the Press.* New York: McGraw-Hill, 1951.
Harper's Pictorial History of the Great Rebellion. New York: Harper, 1886.
Harper's Weekly. 1861–65.
Harwell, Richard, ed. *The Confederate Reader.* New York: Longmans, 1957.
———. *The Union Reader.* New York: Longman's, 1958.
Headley, John W. *Confederate Operations in Canada and New York.* New York: Neale, 1906.
Hearn, C. G. "The Great Locomotive Chase." *Civil War Times Illustrated,* December 1986.
Helper, Hinton R.. *The Impending Crisis of the South: How to Meet It.* N.p.p.: n.p., 1857.
Henderson, G. F. R. *Stonewall Jackson.* 2 vols. Reprint, New York: Smithmark, 1994.
Herold, David E. *The Conspiracy Trial for the Murder of the President and the Attempt to Overthrow the Government by the Assassination of Its Principal Officers.* Reprint, New York: Arno Press, 1972.
Hinton, Richard J. *John Brown and His Men.* New York: Arno Press, 1968.
Illinois Historical Society records.
Jackman, John S. *Diary of a Confederate Soldier.* Columbia: University of South Carolina Press, 1990.
Journal of the Southern Historical Society. 52 vols.
Katcher, Philip. *Confederate Forces of the Civil War.* London: Arms and Armour, 1990.
———. *Great Gambles of the Civil War.* London: Arms and Armour, 1995.
———. *Union Forces of the Civil War.* London: Arms and Armour, 1989.
Klement, Frank L. *Dark Lanterns.* Baton Rouge: Louisiana State University Press, 1989.
Leech, Margaret. *Reveille in Washington.* New York: Harper, 1941.
Logan, John A. *The Great Conspiracy.* New York: n.p., 1886.
Lord, Francis A. *Civil War Collector's Encyclopedia.* 4 vols. Reprint, Salem, N.H.: Ayer, n.d.

Lossing, Benjamin J., ed. *Harper's Encyclopedia of U.S. History.* 19 vols. New York: Harper, 1901.

———. *Matthew Brady's Illustrated History of the Civil War.* Reprint, New York: Grammercy Press, 1994.

———. *Pictorial Field Book of the Civil War.* New Haven: n.p., 1878.

Luraghi, Raimondo. *A History of the Confederate Navy.* Annapolis: Naval Institute Press, 1996.

McElroy, Joseph. *Jefferson Davis.* 2 vols. New York: Harper, 1937.

Markle, Donald E. *Spies and Spymasters of the Civil War.* New York: Hippocrene, 1993.

Martin, Samuel J. *The Road to Glory.* Indianapolis: Guild, 1991.

Miers, Earl S., ed. *Lincoln Day by Day.* 3 vols. Washington, D.C.: Lincoln Sesquicentennial Commission, 1960.

Military Order of the Loyal Legion of the United States. 54 vols. Reprint, Wilmington, Del.: Broadfoot, 1993–95.

Moore, Frank, ed. *The Rebellion Record: A Diary of American Events.* 11 vols. and supplement. New York: Putnam's, 1861–68; Van Nostrand, 1864–68.

Morgan, Sarah. *The Civil War Diary of a Southern Woman.* Athens: University of Georgia Press, 1991.

North Carolina Historical Review. Vol. 14.

National Cyclopedia of American Biography. 69 vols. Reprint, Ann Arbor: University Microfilms, 1967.

Nevins, Alans. *Ordeal of the Union.* 2 vols. New York: Scribner's, 1947.

———. *The War for the Union.* 4 vols. New York: Scribner's, 1959–71.

New Orleans Picayune. 1902.

New Orleans Medical and Surgical Journal. 1844–62.

Nicolay, John G., and John Hay. *Abraham Lincoln: A History.* 10 vols. New York: Century, 1886.

Perry, Milton F. *Infernal Machines: The Story of Confederate Submarine and Mine Warfare.* Baton Rouge: University of Louisiana Press, 1964.

Philadelphia Inquirer. 1962.

Pinkerton, Allan. *The Spy of the Rebellion.* Reprint, Lincoln: University of Nebraska Press, 1989.

Ploski, Harry A., and James Williams, eds. *The Negro Almanac.* New York: Wiley, 1983.

Pollard, E. A. *The Lost Cause.* Reprint, New York: Grammercy Press, 1994.

Poore, Ben Purley, ed. *The Conspiracy Trial for the Murder of the President.* 3 vols. Reprint, New York: Arno Press, 1972.

———. *Life and Public Services of Ambrose E. Burnside.* Providence, R.I.: n.p., 1882.

———. *Life of U. S. Grant.* New York: Century, 1892.

Randall, James G. *Constitutional Problems under Lincoln.* Springfield, Ill.: Abraham Lincoln Association, 1943.

———. *Lincoln, the President.* 4 vols. New York: Dodd, 1945–55.

Report on the Conduct of the War. Washington, D.C.: Government Printing Office, 1865.

Richardson, Albert. *The Secret Service.* Hartford: American, 1865.

Richmond Examiner. 1862.

Robinson, William Morrison. *The Confederate Privateers.* Columbia: University of South Carolina Press, 1928.

Roller, David C., and Robert W. Twyman, eds. *The Encyclopedia of Southern History.* Baton Rouge: University of Louisiana Press, 1968.

Scharf, J. Thomas. *History of the Confederate Navy.* Reprint, New York: Grammercy Press, 1996.

Sears, Stephen W. "The Great Locomotive Chase." *American Heritage,* 1991.

The Soldier in Our Civil War. Reprint, Jackson: University of Mississippi Press, 1995.

Smith, Arthur D. *Old Fuss and Feathers.* New York: Greystone, 1937.

Spencer, Warren F. *The Confederate Navy in Europe.* University: University of Alabama Press, 1983.

Stanley, Dorothy, ed. *The Autobiography of Sir Henry Morton Stanley.* Boston: Houghton Mifflin, 1922.

Starkey, Larry. *Wilkes Booth Came to Washington.* New York: Random, 1976.

The Statistical History of the United States from Colonial Times to the Present. New York: Basic Books, 1976.

Stern, Philip Van Doren. *An End to Valor.* Reprint, New York: Bonanza, 1958.

———. *The Confederate Navy.* Reprint, New York: Da Capo Press, 1992.

———. *Secret Missions of the Civil War.* Reprint, New York: Bonanza, 1959.

Thomason, John W. *Jeb Stuart.* London: Scribner's, 1930.

Tidwell, William A. *April '65.* Kent, Ohio: Kent State University Press, 1995.

Trout, Robert J., *They Followed the Plume.* Mechanicsburg, Pa.: Stackpole, 1993.

U.S. Navy Department. *Official Records of the Union and Confederate Navies in the War of the Rebellion.* 31 vols. Washington, D.C.: Government Printing Office, 1894–1927.

U.S. War Department. *The War of the Rebellion: A Compilation of the Official Records of the Union and Confederate Armies.* 128 vols. Washington, D.C.: Government Printing Office, 1880–1901.

Vandiver, Frank. *Jubal's Raid.* New York: McGraw-Hill, 1960.

Van Dusen, Glyndon G. *William Henry Seward.* New York: Oxford, 1967.

Welles, Gideon. *Diary.* 2 vols. New York: Houghton Mifflin, 1911.

———. *Lincoln and Seward.* New York: Sheldon, 1874.

Welch, Peter. *Irish Green and Union Blue.* New York: Fordham University Press, 1986.

Williams, E. Cort. "The Cruise of 'The Black Terror.'" *Ohio MOLLUS,* Vol. 3.

Wilson, Francis, *John Wilkes Booth.* New York: Blom, 1972.

Wilson, John A. *Adventures of Alf Wilson.* Toledo: Blade, 1880.

Wise, Stephen R. *Lifeline of the Confederacy.* Columbia: University of South Carolina Press, 1988.

Woodward, W. E. *Meet General Grant.* New York: Literary Guild, 1928.

Index

Illustrations are noted by **boldface.**